THERE IS HOP

"There will be o...
said the doctor.

But would Sharon live to see them? Lucille Gardner clung to that hope as she recalled the terrible auto crash that had stripped the 15-year-old of all but her very life.

Mrs. Gardner recalls:
"When her father and I brought her home—a terrified creature, almost more animal than human—we faced a tortuous climb up an unmarked trail. . . . With painful slowness we led her through the maze of all her unknowns—walking, talking, toilet training, controlling her emotions, learning her abc's all over again— and experienced with her a unique joy in each accomplishment.

"Sharon experienced the hurt and loneliness of rejection by her peers, the agony of struggling to learn fifth-grade reading and arithmetic while her former classmates finished college. Yet each problem or hurt became a building block of growth. . . ."

There IS Hope

LUCILLE GARDNER

CHOICE BOOKS
THE BEST IN FAMILY READING
P. O. Box 706
Goshen, IN 46526
We Welcome Your Response

David C. Cook Publishing Co.
ELGIN, ILLINOIS—WESTON, ONTARIO
LA HABRA, CALIFORNIA

David C. Cook Publishing Co., Elgin, IL 60120
Printed in the United States of America

First printing—August, 1976
Second printing—December, 1976

Library of Congress Catalog Number: 76-4615
ISBN: 0-912692-89-8

This book is dedicated to all who struggle to help a loved one considered hopeless by society. My earnest prayer is that you may receive from these pages the priceless gift of hope, and the certain conviction that "with God all things are possible."

TABLE OF CONTENTS

PREFACE

On November 10, 1961, our 15-year-old Sharon reminded me as she left for school: "I'll be late getting home, Mom, because of the game after school." She was *very* late—two and one-half months—and the girl we brought back then bore little resemblance to the pretty, vivacious honor-roll student who left that crisp November morning.

When Sharon was crossing a street after the game she was struck by a car and severely injured. For ten weeks she wavered between life and death; then, stripped of knowledge and memory, and reduced to a mental infant, she started the long road back to conscious living.

When her father and I brought her home—a terrified creature, almost more animal than human—we faced a torturous climb up an unmarked trail. We inched our way, constantly led and sustained by a very real, though unseen, Guide.

With painful slowness, we led her through the maze of all her unknowns—walking, talking, toilet training, controlling her emotions, learning ABC's—and experienced, with her, a unique joy in each accomplishment.

Sharon experienced the hurt and loneliness of rejection by her peers, the agony of struggling to learn fifth-grade reading and arithmetic while her former classmates finished college. Yet each problem or hurt became a building block of growth.

Perhaps the greatest growth that has come to all of us is the certain knowledge that man's impossibilities become possible when human love provides the channel through which God's love can freely flow to transform human tragedy to divine blessing.

1

"There Will Be Other Christmases"

I PAUSED AT THE DOOR of room 300 to gaze at the gaily dressed Christmas tree on the chest of drawers in the corner. All the packages lay beneath it—still unopened. I struggled to master my disappointment, greeted the nurse, then walked over to the bed and smiled at our Sharon. "Merry Christmas, Dear." The wide gray eyes beneath the skull cap that covered her bandaged head stared back at me, but I could detect no change in her thin, pale expressionless face. There was no recognition in those dull eyes.

My hands felt cold and damp as I held a package out to her: "It's a present for you, Darling, a Christmas present."

Still the vacant look remained unchanged. I laid the gift on the bed and watched. Every nerve tensed as her hand slowly moved toward it. Her fingers touched the bow for an instant, feeling its soft smooth surface.

"Open it, Dear, it's for you."

I held my breath and waited. She moved her head a little and her eyes stared straight at me, but still she seemed not to hear or to be aware of my voice. Her hand moved from the ribbon to the feeding tube that protruded from her nose, fingering it while the package fell to the floor.

I sank into the chair beside the bed, desperately clutching at what was left of my hope.

The strains of *Silent Night, Holy Night* drifting into the room only intensified my heartache and frustration. Christmas, the day of glorious fulfillment! How I had yearned for this day to fulfill the hope I had clung to through the 44 anguished days in which Sharon had waged her battle for life.

Someone came into the room. I felt a light touch on my shoulder, and looked up into the compassionate eyes of our family physician. "There will be other Christmases." His voice trembled with emotion. He patted my shoulder again; then turned and walked out.

Long moments passed before the special nurse broke the silence: "Sharon has been quite calm today. She seems on the verge of 'waking up' any minute."

Yes, I thought, that's what they keep telling me. But when? I felt the strain tightening every fiber in my body. How much more could my taut nerves stand?

The unanswered question still hung in the air when I heard my husband's heavy footsteps, then Charley's coaxing voice: "Come on, Honey. Les is getting restless. We'll come back later."

I settled myself in the car before answering our son's eager question: "Did she look at the gift, Mom?"

"No, Dear, but it's such a relief to see her quiet rather than still tossing and screaming. The nurse says she appears to be on the verge of 'waking up' any minute."

"It seems I've heard that song before." His dejected voice held all the disappointment he felt that even Christmas had brought no change in his 15-year-old twin sister.

I sensed that Charley, too, was struggling to control his emotions. Had we all secretly hoped for a Christmas miracle?

All three of us made an effort to keep conversation going during the six-mile ride to the home of Stella and Dick Brown, our daughter and son-in-law.

Four-year-old Rickey and two-year-old Sheri bounded out to the car, greeting each of us with a hug and a "hi" and asking in the same breath if we had brought them any presents. Then a battle ensued to keep the wrappings on until we got inside the house.

We stepped over toys and wrappings and eventually found a place to sit just about the same time that Rickey and Sheri finished opening their gifts. Then they scrambled over and tried to take the ones we were still holding. What a perfect Christmas this would be if only Sharon could be enjoying it here with us, I thought.

Pictures flashed through my mind of our intelligent, effervescent daughter who had kissed me good-bye that morning—could it be only 45 days ago? It seemed like many years, yet I remembered every detail of that tragic November day. . . .

Sounds from somewhere in the house penetrated my consciousness, and I struggled to focus my eyes on the luminous dial of the clock on our dresser. It showed 7 o'clock. I didn't dare let myself go back to sleep, but it felt good to just lie quietly a few minutes.

13

Then I slipped out of bed, put on my bathrobe, and tiptoed out, closing the door behind me. I started past Sharon's bedroom, then noticed her light through the crack in the door, just as I heard her cheery greeting: "Hi, Mom, how're you?"

I opened the door and watched her rummage through her closet, then select a skirt and vest that she had made in sewing class.

"I'm fine, Dear, but I'm anxious to know how you are. You sound awfully perky to have been so miserable the last couple of days. It couldn't be partly a cover-up to persuade me to let you go back to school today, could it?"

"No, really, Mom, I feel fine." She flashed me a persuasive, impish grin. "That's the one good thing about the stomach flu, it doesn't last long; but, boy, is it miserable while you have it!"

I watched her reflection in the mirror as she finished dressing and combed her short, light brown hair. She twirled a couple of times, with a critical glance at her slender figure in the mirror, then she brushed past me as she headed for the bathroom.

I tried one weak protest: "I had expected you to stay home today, since it's Friday, and that would give you the weekend to really get over the flu."

"It will be tough enough to make the honor roll after missing two days, Mom. I can't miss another one." Her gray eyes danced with excitement. "Besides, one of our most important football games is today. Really, Mom, don't worry, I'll be fine."

I started to suggest that at least she should come home right after school and not stay for the game, but she had won me over and I said nothing. Many times in the months

14

ahead my silence on this occasion would come back to haunt me.

I hurried into the living room and shook the long lump in the sleeping bag on the sofa, where Les had been sleeping since our home had become a two-family residence. How different our twins are, I thought. Sharon rarely has to be called, but it often requires a strong arm and some sharp verbal digs to uproot Les. Slowly a head emerged. One look at his pale face and a sigh escaped me: "Oh, no, not you too."

He nodded. "I've been sick all night." He burrowed deeper into the sleeping bag.

My heart sank as I thought: Is this flu bug going to hit all of us? The prospect seemed almost more than I could face. Just managing to keep everything under control with nine people in the house had seemed an impossible task many times during the last five months. I dearly loved every member of our extended family—Stella and Dick Brown and their three adorable children, Rickey, Sheri, and six-week-old Michael; but we'd all surely be glad when they could move into their new home.

I tucked the sleeping bag around Les' shoulders and returned to the kitchen wondering what, if anything, I could do to keep the flu from spreading to the rest of the family.

I dished some hot oatmeal for Sharon, and she ate it, keeping one eye on the clock, then gathered her books and started off. Halfway to the front door, she ran back, planted a light kiss on my cheek, and said in her quick, emphatic manner: "Mom, you look awfully beat. You'd better get some rest or you will get sick yourself."

She went on: "Don't worry about the house. It doesn't

15

do any good anyway, because the kids mess it up quicker than you can clean it. I'll help you with the housework tomorrow.''

The day sped by faster than I realized. Just before dark, I hurried out to bring in the clothes from the line. I folded the towels and put them away, then started into Sharon's room with several of her unironed blouses. I tried her door before remembering that she now kept it locked when she was away to keep Rickey and Sheri from disturbing her "valuables."

I heard the front door open, and the happy shouts from Rickey and Sheri: "Daddy, Daddy." Then Rickey's excited voice: "Grandpa brought us some cookies." I hadn't realized that Grandpa was home. Then I heard him talking and Stella laughing, and knew they were all in the living room.

I took the key off the nail at the top of the door facing, unlocked Sharon's door, and deposited the blouses on top of the bulging basket of unironed clothes in her closet. Would she ever catch up on her ironing? I wondered. Too often she waited until she had nothing left to wear before digging into the pile and ironing one garment at a time as she needed it. Of course, she really had little spare time, I reasoned. She studied so hard and she spent so much time with the drama group, the spirit committee, and practicing cheerleading at school, as well as taking part in the youth activities at church. I smiled to myself as I thought: How she loves life and everything connected with it!

I locked the door behind me and was replacing the key when I heard the telephone. I started toward it, but Stella reached it first. She talked quietly for a few minutes. Then she hung up the phone, dashed into the back part of the house, and returned with her coat on. She whispered to Dick, and the two of them rushed out the front door, mumbling something about being back in a short while. Moments later Stella poked her head in the door and called her dad. He went out with her, and I stood debating whether I should follow them and demand an explanation for their strange actions. Then suddenly I heard the car drive away.

Something is wrong, and they are keeping it from me, I thought. I went into the bedroom where Les had moved to in midmorning, and inquired: "Shouldn't Sharon be home by now?"

He looked at the clock and then answered: "She'll be here before long. She's probably with Lynda and Joanne, and they poke along when they're talking. Where's Dad and everybody?"

I told him about their strange behavior, and he said, "Don't worry, Mom; there's probably some simple explanation for their crazy antics, and Sharon will show up any minute now."

I struggled to control my growing fear and remain calm.

Sheri and Rickey had come into the room and started to climb up by Les. They couldn't quite understand why I stopped them.

"Come on," I coaxed. "I'll read a book to you." They climbed up beside me on the living room sofa and we were lamenting poor baby bear's broken chair when the telephone rang again.

My hand shook as I picked it up. An unfamiliar voice answered my "hello" and asked: "Is this Mrs. Gardner?" When I replied, it went on: "This is the hospital calling. Your daughter, Sharon, is here. She has been hit

17

by a car. Can you come to the emergency room right away?''

''How badly is she hurt?'' The words came out slowly; I felt panic-stricken, but knew I had to keep calm.

''We don't know yet.''

A thousand thoughts tumbled around in my brain, and I knew I didn't make sense as I tried to explain that my husband, daughter, and son-in-law were no doubt on their way to the hospital.

The voice now had an anxious tone as it questioned: ''Are you ill, Mrs. Gardner?''

''No, I'm not ill.'' My words rushed out. ''But Sharon was hit by a car once before, and that time I arrived at the scene while she still lay in the street. I guess they wanted to spare me that this time.''

When I paused another anxious question came over the wire: ''Are you alone, Mrs. Gardner?''

''No, my son and grandchildren are here. I'll try to find someone to bring me right away.''

I went into the bedroom and told Les. He covered his face with his hands, and choked on his words: ''Oh no, Mom, not again!''

''Do you think you can manage the children, if I can get a neighbor to take me to the hospital?''

''Of course, Mom, don't give them another thought.''

When I got to the hospital, Stella, Dick, and Mrs. Zambetti, the mother of Sharon's close friend, Lynda, filled me in on what had happened.

Sharon and two friends had been crossing the street near their school when a small sports car raced through the intersection. Somehow the others had managed to jump back in time to avoid being hit, but the car struck Sharon

18

with such force that it threw her into the air, then caught her falling body and dragged her, head down, for some distance.

Charley glanced up as I walked in, and the agony in his face cut like a knife. "She's unconscious and has severe head injuries." His voice broke, and he waited a minute before going on: "They can't reach our doctor."

Just then one of the nurses came over to us. "An excellent neurosurgeon just left here a few minutes ago. He left all his instruments, because he intended to return. Would you like for us to see if we can get him back right away?"

"Oh, yes, please do," Charley answered quickly.

Each second now seemed like hours. Finally the nurse told us: "The neurosurgeon is on his way back."

Then she asked: "Would you like to see Sharon?"

Charley shook his head "no"; but I said "yes," and she led me into the room where Sharon lay. I gasped as I looked at her. Her hair was matted with blood, her eyes were open with a fixed stare, and her body had a strange, rigid look. I leaned over her, took her hand and felt her stiff fingers. Looking into her staring eyes I said softly: "You're going to be all right, Sharon. It's Mother, Honey. I'm here, and I'm going to stay with you, Dear. You're going to be all right."

All my being cried out silently, in anguish, to God: "Oh, let me get through to her. Please, dear God, let her somehow know I'm here, and that You're here with us, too. God, we both need Your presence so much right now."

I turned away with calm peace flooding through me, that peace which is beyond human understanding.

2

Moment by Moment

AFTER LEAVING THE EMERGENCY ROOM, I walked down
the hall, A young girl in a candy-striper uniform came up
to me. She wiped her eyes, red from crying, and blurted
out between sobs: "Oh, Mrs. Gardner, it's so awful. I'm
so sorry about Sharon. I'm Eileen. I've known Sharon
since we used to play dolls together over at Lynda's. Oh,
it's just awful."

I thanked her and walked on, thinking it strange that I
should feel so calm. I didn't feel at all like crying. I felt as
though I should comfort Eileen.

The four of us, Charley, Dick, Stella, and I, sat quietly
and waited, each intent on his own thoughts. The nurse
told us the neurosurgeon had arrived and was examining
Sharon, and that they had also located our family physician and he would be at the hospital soon.

I heard loud screams from somewhere down the corridor and vaguely wondered about it. Then I heard a

familiar voice speak my name and looked up to see Harriet Dean, who lived across the street from us and worked on the hospital switchboard.

"I heard those screams and feared it was you. I'm so relieved to see you're all right. If there's anything at all I can do for you, please let me know. We'll all be praying for Sharon and the family."

She started to leave, then came back to ask: "Why don't you come on down to the main lobby? This is such a miserable place to wait. They'll bring you word as soon as there is any."

Gratefully, we followed her and found comfortable seats. We sipped the coffee she brought us and waited.

After what seemed a very long time, we saw a self-assured young man walking briskly toward us. He introduced himself, then quickly went on: "From the severity of Sharon's head injuries and the rigidity of her body, we feel that exploratory brain surgery—a craniotomy—should be performed immediately. We would usually wait until we have some indication of the area of damage, but because of the evidence of possible brain stem injury, and the probability of bleeding, resulting in clots forming in the brain, we feel time is of utmost importance. We hope to be able to relieve some of the pressure. However, the surgery may not accomplish anything; and there is the possibility that if we wait we can get an indication of the damaged area. The decision is up to you."

Charley and I looked at each other. Neither of us spoke; 25 years of sharing each other's lives made words unnecessary. "We want to do everything possible for our daughter," Charley said. "We have faith in your judgment, Doctor. Go ahead with the operation."

I added: "I know you'll do everything you can for our Sharon."

His clear, gray eyes looked deep into mine, and his firm, confident voice had a soft, almost humble quality as he said: "With God's help, I will."

Tears filled my eyes, not from grief, but from deep gratitude for this assurance that our daughter was in good hands.

Charley put a comforting arm around my shoulders and squeezed my hand, and again we sat down to wait.

We repeated the doctor's words to Stella and Dick, and then they left to return home.

Friends who had heard the news began to arrive and Harriet ushered us into a private room that opened off the lobby. There, surrounded and comforted by those who loved us and understood, we waited out the long hours.

Our family doctor brought the report to us. His compassion showed in his face and his voice. "Sharon survived the operation, but her condition is extremely critical. Each hour she lives gives her that much more chance to make it. You count the hours until several days have passed, then you count the days until a week or more has gone by, then you can assume that she has a fair chance for life. She will require round-the-clock special nurses; they're trying to locate one for tonight."

We relayed the report to those who waited with us, and expressed our deep gratitude. Then we took the elevator to the third floor, found room 300, and waited silently for its new occupant to arrive.

We had braced ourselves for what was to come, but nothing could have prepared us for the shock as they wheeled our daughter into the room. Horror gripped me as

23

I looked at her. Her head, even allowing for the many layers of bandages, appeared swollen twice its normal size. Her face, what little showed outside the bandages, was a swollen, bruised mass, her features scarcely recognizable. From her nose protruded a stomach tube, from her mouth a black rubber airway. A catheter had been inserted, and a bottle of IV fluid hung at the end of the bed.

We stood in numb silence in the dim room, painfully aware that at any moment the fragile thread that held her life might break.

One of the hospital staff came to tell us that they had been unable to locate a registered nurse on such short notice, and so they had engaged a practical nurse for this night only.

When she arrived, I insisted that Charley go on home. I knew he needed rest for the ordeal of the days ahead, and our son needed him at home.

The nurse took a long look at Sharon, then glanced at me. The look of compassion in her eyes, and the gentle lines of her face gave me comfort and assurance.

I sat down by the bed, and once more the compelling desire possessed me to get through to Sharon. I leaned close to her and slowly and distinctly told her: "You're going to be all right, Sharon. I'm here with you, Honey. You'll be all right, Sharon. I'll be right here with you. I'm not going to leave you."

As I spoke I gazed intently at the tiny bit of eyeball that I could see through the narrow slit at the bottom of her swollen eyelid.

I longed for some sign that she knew of my presence. Reason argued the absurdity of hoping for any response from her, but my heart would not accept the fact. Again, all my being cried out to God.

I felt an arm around me, and then the nurse's soft voice suggested: "Tell her to blink her eyelid if she can hear you."

Excited, I once again leaned over Sharon and slowly urged: "If you can hear me, Sharon, please blink your eyelid."

A long moment passed, then the narrow slit of eyeball disappeared as the eyelid covered it for an instant.

I looked tearfully up into the nurse's eyes. "She did blink, didn't she?"

Her smiling nod gave the confirmation I needed, and I found it difficult to keep from shouting as I said: "She heard me. She blinked her eye to tell me that she heard me, and that she's going to be all right."

My thoughts went back to that other time when she had comforted me with those words. I remembered every detail of the experience as though it had happened only yesterday, instead of five years ago. That time she had been injured when a car struck her while she rode her bicycle across an intersection near our home. I arrived at the scene while she still lay in the street, one leg at a right angle to the rest of her body, her face bruised and bloody, her eyes wide open but blinded from shock.

I knelt by her and my voice trembled as I told her: "It's Mother. I'm here with you, Honey."

She had answered in a firm, reassuring tone. "I can hear you, Mother, but I can't see you. Don't you worry, Mother; I'll be all right."

All the way to the hospital in the ambulance she had kept reassuring me: "Don't you worry, Mother. I'm

25

going to be all right. You aren't worrying, are you?''

"She must love you very much to be worrying about you instead of herself," the ambulance attendant had remarked.

Then, the test and x-rays had showed no severe injuries other than her broken thigh. The doctors performed a pinning operation and assured me that after some six months she should be able to walk normally again. Extreme shock had caused the blindness, and by morning she was able to see again.

No other injuries surfaced, and I knew no plausible reason for the extreme nervous reaction I suffered. Night after night when I tried to sleep, I tossed and turned, reliving the nightmare of screaming sirens, anxious faces, broken bones, and blood.

Charley was 2500 miles away, at a family reunion. I had to conquer this, somehow, by myself, I thought. Then I realized my error. If I had any true conviction that God looks after His own constantly, and especially at times of great stress, then I'd better act like it and trust Him to help me through it.

The nightmare disappeared, replaced by the definite assurance of God's moment-by-moment guidance. I recognized my partnership with God in caring for my family. If I faithfully carried out my duties as wife and mother, then I could leave the rest to God, with the certain knowledge that no matter how far away my husband or my children might be, none of them could ever be beyond His love and protection.

Now I wondered: Had Sharon been injured previously to strengthen us for this ordeal? I needed the lessons learned from that earlier accident to support me now. I sat in the semidarkness, pondering the thought, while I watched the nurse draw out mucus from Sharon's throat with the suction machine. A desperate struggle still raged within me. One part of me wanted to be submissive to God's will, and the other desperately wanted Sharon to live.

Finally I prayed silently but fervently: "Oh, dear God, You know how much we love Sharon, how we long to keep her with us. Thank You for answering my prayer and giving me the assurance, through the movement of her eyelid, that she is aware of my presence. I want to be submissive to Your will, Lord, but oh, how difficult it is to face the thought of losing Sharon! Yet I know You love her with a love far beyond our human love, and that even death cannot separate her from You or Your love. That thought comforts me so much now, Lord, and gives me the strength to say 'Thy Will Be Done.' "

I didn't realize that someone had come into the room until I felt a gentle touch on my shoulder and looked up into the face of our close friend and former pastor, Rev. Woodrow Davis. His eyes mirrored his concern, and the tone of his voice revealed even more than his words: "An hour has passed and she still lives. Pauline and I will sit in the lobby all night, to be close if you need us. Of course, we will spend the time praying."

My feeble thanks poorly conveyed my deep gratitude.

The nurse had finished with the suction machine by the time Rev. Davis quietly left. Once more I repeated to Sharon: "You're going to be all right, Sharon. I know you're going to be all right, Honey." My voice had an even deeper conviction than before. She would be all right, whether God willed for her to remain with us, fully whole, or mentally and physically handicapped, or whether death claimed her.

Then I sat quietly by her side, once more absorbed in memory, recalling how we had worked together with the Davis family to establish a church in a section of the city where one was badly needed. I remembered how we grew in maturity as the church grew, for we learned to depend on God for solutions to problems.

As I looked at my unconscious daughter, I thanked God for those experiences that had strengthened my faith. I watched the nurse's face as she felt Sharon's pulse, trying to interpret her expression.

"How is it?" I asked.

She waited a long moment before answering, and my heart started pounding.

"It's just about the same."

Neither her answer nor her expression told me much. I glanced at my watch: 1 a.m. Only seven hours had passed since the call came from the hospital, but what an eternity it seemed!

I heard the door open, and watched Rev. Davis walk over to me. With a quickening pulse I heard his words: "Another hour has passed, and she still lives."

He left quietly; but another, very real, though unseen, Presence made Himself known in the room.

I felt Him in every fiber of my being, and the message He brought stirred the deepest feeling within me: *"Sharon is going to live. She will be all right."*

This definite promise became a firm conviction within me from that moment. It defied explanation in human terms, but I needed no explanation.

The minutes seemed to go faster now, while a constant kaleidoscope of thoughts flashed through my mind. I discovered things I could do to help the nurse; I held the IV needle steady, helped when the suction machine was used, and helped when she moved Sharon.

Each hour Rev. Davis returned with his message of hope, and each time I felt again the gratitude for their presence and their prayers, but his words had lost their impact. Of course each hour that passed found her still alive, for *she would live; she would get well*.

3

Another Crisis

WHEN I REALIZED IT WAS TIME for the special nurse to go off duty, I felt a real sense of loss and tried and tried to express my appreciation.

"It doesn't seem possible that eight hours ago we were total strangers. While we've struggled to keep Sharon alive, I've felt a closeness to you that I've felt toward few people in my lifetime. I'll always remember your deep concern for Sharon, and your dedicated efforts."

Her voice wavered as she said: "I have a daughter, too. I know you love your girl as much as I do mine."

When the special day nurse arrived I couldn't help but contrast the two. She appeared old, with lean wrinkled face and long thin fingers. Instead of the gentle, compassionate look of our night nurse, her eyes and expression had a stern, hard quality. Her manner, as she put her coat and purse away and came over to the bed to look at Sharon, plainly said, "I'm in charge here."

The two nurses greeted each other by first names, and then went over Sharon's chart together.

I followed the night nurse into the hall when she left, and when I started to tell her good-bye she interrupted me. She spoke in a low tone, and her face had an expression I couldn't quite interpret. "You know, you don't have to keep any special nurse you are not satisfied with; insist on a replacement. You have the right to." I would recall her words in the weeks ahead.

I went downstairs to the cafeteria and ate a hearty breakfast. No wonder the food tastes so good, I thought. I haven't eaten since lunch yesterday, and I've lived a lifetime in between.

The daylight hours passed much faster than the long night ones. Charley came in midmorning and brought me a change of clothing and the morning paper—pointing out the article about Sharon.

"Did you get any sleep, Honey?" I asked.

"A little, at least more than you did." Fatigue showed in his voice. "I'm writing down the names of the callers. They all want us to let them know if there's anything they can do."

"I hope you told each of them that they can do one important thing for us—they can pray."

"Almost everyone told me they were praying for her. Guess we don't realize how many wonderful friends we have until tragedy strikes."

The slurp of the suction machine made conversation difficult, so we walked out into the corridor.

"How's Les? He seemed so miserable from the flu yesterday, and now I know he must be almost beside himself from worrying about Sharon."

"I think he's just about over the flu, but I'm glad to have the excuse that he can't come to the hospital for several days because of the danger of germs. It would be impossible to keep him away otherwise, and he doesn't need to see Sharon as she is now." His voice broke as he went on: "It's almost more than I can do to look at her." He clenched his fist. "The agony of seeing her like this makes me boil at the irresponsible idiot who struck her." His voice rose with each word.

"Calm down, Honey, you're talking too loud."

He lowered his voice a little, but his face was red with anger. "I went to the police station this morning and looked at the accident report. It shows that the brakes on the car that struck her gave no resistance when tested. The policemen said a lot of the young sports car drivers think it's smart to drive without brakes, and to shift gears to slow or stop the car. A young girl about 19 years old was driving the car that struck Sharon. Stella said she heard someone at the accident scene last night say the car that struck Sharon had been racing with the other car." He was almost shouting again, and paced the corridor as he talked.

I wanted to tell him about my definite assurance that Sharon would live, but his mood stopped me. I thought of the tremendous load on his shoulders now. His insurance job, in itself, demanded so much of his time, and now all the business details connected with the accident would absorb many hours. Yet Les needed all the time my husband could possibly spare. My heart ached for him, but I didn't know how to help.

We stood a moment in silence, then he squeezed my arm and walked quickly to the elevator.

As I stood watching him, a long-loved phrase came to mind: "All things work together for good," and I thought: What a blessing it is that Stella's family still lives with us. They'll be such a comfort to Charley and Les.

The long hours passed slowly while I helped with the nursing tasks, talking to Sharon's still form as I worked. Throughout the day, a steady stream of friends came to the hospital. At the end of the day I had entered 34 names on the visitors' list I was keeping.

Among the most welcome callers was one of the nurses from emergency. "I couldn't sleep all night thinking about Sharon. I have teenagers, too, so I could understand your suffering. Oh, how I hope and pray she will be all right." I felt amazed that she should be so concerned about Sharon, considering all the severely injured persons she cares for each day.

By the time the night nurse came on at 11, my dulled senses reminded me that 40 hours was about the maximum I could go without sleep. I took the blanket and pillow that Charley had brought from home, exacted a promise from the nurse that she would call me in the event of any change in Sharon's condition, then walked to the end of the corridor and curled up on a four-foot wooden bench and sank into deep sleep. Six hours later I awakened, refreshed in mind and body. I realized that it was Sunday, and a comforting feeling came over me as I pictured our Sunday school class praying for us, and also realized that Rev. Nastari would include an earnest petition for Sharon and the rest of our family in his prayer during the morning worship service.

I washed my face, and combed my hair in the rest room, and then walked rapidly down the hall to room 300.

The room seemed deadly still. The nurse sat at the far side writing on her chart. The motionless body on the bed, with the tubes protruding from her nose and the huge bandaged head looked even more grotesque in the dim light. A groan caught in my throat and I bit my lips until I tasted blood, as I struggled to control my emotions. Then God answered my whispered prayer for strength, and I felt again the peace and comfort of His presence. I walked to the side of the bed, felt under the covers for Sharon's cold, stiff hand, then leaned over close to her. "Good morning, Honey. I'll be right here with you." Two tiny portions of eyeball stared at me.

Can she hear me? Does she know me? Is she at least vaguely aware of my presence?

The questions hung in the air—unanswerable.

I went to the cafeteria soon after it opened. I knew that if I was to maintain my health and be of maximum benefit to Sharon, I had to have regular meals as well as a few hours of sleep each night.

I had been back from breakfast only a few minutes when Eileen, Sharon's candy-striper friend, came in. I told her I felt sure Sharon had been aware of my presence that first night, and that she had blinked her eyelid for me. "Maybe I can get her to blink for you." I leaned over Sharon's still form and looked straight into the tiny portion of eyeball below the swollen eyelids.

"Sharon, Honey. Your friend Eileen is here to see you. Can you blink for us this morning? Try to blink your eyelid so we'll know you hear us."

We held our breath and waited. "Blink for us, please. You're going to be all right, Sharon."

Again we waited in silence, watching for the slightest

35

movement. After a long moment, the eyeballs disappeared for an instant, and Eileen and I, too overcome with emotion to speak, hugged each other.

In an awed whisper Eileen told me: "I got up early this morning to go to mass and pray for Sharon. God has already answered part of my prayer. Lynda, Joanne and I are going to keep a diary for Sharon while she's in the hospital, so she won't miss out on anything. Boy, will I have something to put in it this morning!"

With afternoon visiting hours, several of Sharon's school friends arrived and I ushered them over to her bedside. "Talk to her just as you would if she could answer you," I suggested.

They tried, but instead of their usual happy, excited conversation, they spoke haltingly in hushed tones.

Lynda and Joanne came in, and in a shaking voice Lynda said, "We're praying for you to get well, Sharon. We miss you so much." Her voice broke, and she walked quickly from the room.

Through that night and all the dark nights and days since then I felt again and again the strength of the prayers of Sharon's peers, and those of our friends and loved ones, as well as countless strangers.

Soon Sharon's unconscious body was no longer completely motionless. Her right side started jerking and her arm shot out in wild spastic movements. Hard as it had been to see her so deadly still, I found the uncontrolled movements even more disturbing. Her right side remained rigid; the doctors told me that even the muscles in her face on that side were paralyzed.

Monday evening I looked up from my task of helping the nurse straighten the bedclothes to see Les come quietly into the room. His pale drawn face and the pained look in his eyes cut through me. They told me plainer than any words his agony during the long three days since I had seen him. Since early childhood he had considered himself Sharon's protector, ready to fight anyone or anything that threatened her.

He walked slowly toward the bed, stood for an instant in silence, then before either the nurse or I could grab him, his tall, lanky body crashed to the floor.

Nurses came running into the room, and soon they were working over him with smelling salts and wet cloths. I watched him for what seemed like an eternity. Then slowly his eyes opened, his gaze met mine, and he whispered, "I'm OK, Mom." In a few minutes he tried to get up, insisting, "I'm all right, Mom."

Instead of letting him get up, the nurses helped him into a wheelchair and sent him to the emergency department for X rays and a checkup. To my great relief no broken bones or other problems showed up, and the doctors assured me his extreme reaction had been caused by his weakened physical condition following his bout with the flu.

"Mother, it wasn't seeing Sharon unconscious with all those tubes and bandages that hit me so hard," Les later explained. "It was the spastic movements. Will her arm always shoot out wildly like that?"

"I'm sure it won't," I answered. But deep inside I wondered.

Soon we faced another complication. Sharon's fever started rising, and I grew more and more apprehensive as her flesh felt hotter and hotter until it almost burned my fingers when I touched her. Then I learned why—the part of her brain that regulated the body temperature had been damaged. Her "thermostat" no longer worked.

With rubber gloves to protect our hands from the extreme cold, the nurses and I dipped washcloths in iced alcohol, then placed them on her burning body; a few seconds later we removed them, steaming from heat, and repeated the process. For five days and nights we worked frantically without resting, in order to stem the fever and keep her alive.

I knew that such uncontrolled temperature, even without the massive damage already apparent, could cause complete brain death, but I wouldn't let myself dwell on that thought. I had God's promise, and I knew I could depend on it.

Charley didn't share my assurance, and with each daily visit I sensed his deepening despair and frustration. The physical activity of caring for Sharon gave me a satisfaction that he could not share. He could only stand helplessly and watch. In so many ways he bore the greater burden.

When I'd ask how things were going at home his short replies: "OK," or "Oh, we're managing," told me very little. Then once when I asked him about their meals, he mentioned that several casseroles, salads, and desserts had been brought to the house by neighbors and friends at different times. "The speed at which those casseroles disappeared indicated we were all tired of peanut butter sandwiches."

Well-balanced meals had always been a must for Charley. His body required them. Dick, whose job included hard physical labor, and Les, needed them also. But how could Stella manage all the extra responsibility now placed on her? I thought with a pang how tired she had looked since Mike's birth.

The answer came from a totally unexpected source.

One evening Mr. McGuire, manager of Charley's insurance company, came by the hospital to see me. "All of us at the office want to express our deep sympathy and concern in a tangible manner," he said. "We discussed ways that we might do this and have decided that each family represented on our office staff—agents, managers and office personnel, will take turns preparing meals and sending them to your home. We know Stella has her hands more than full now, and we can at least relieve her of that responsibility."

I didn't thank him; my thankfulness was too deep for words. But I'm sure he sensed the depths of my gratitude.

For several weeks, delicious, hot meals were delivered each evening. After all those in Charley's office had taken a turn, one of the neighboring insurance offices followed the same procedure. Then members of the executive board of our PTA sent meals on successive nights. Often Charley brought me some when he came to the hospital.

Gradually Sharon's fever subsided; the iced cloths no longer steamed, and finally we put them aside. On Friday evening, one week after the accident, the nurse smiled as she looked at the thermometer. Our daughter's temperature was almost normal; another crisis had passed.

Then suddenly I realized something I hadn't even been aware of earlier. The spastic movements had ceased. She appeared to be peacefully sleeping. My heart overflowed with thanksgiving, and my sleep that night was deep and refreshing.

4

As a Mustard Seed

THE NEXT MORNING as I sat beside the bed watching Sharon, I felt again the compulsion to try to get through to her—to strengthen my hope that live brain cells remained despite the fearful fever. I waited until both doctors had finished their rounds, because I remembered too vividly their earlier reaction when I told them: "I feel sure Sharon is aware of my presence, and at times I can get through to her."

Our family physician patted my shoulder and looked at me the way one does a child who has just related some elaborate story about her doll. Both he and the neurosurgeon told me they wished they could believe me, but they knew it wasn't possible.

As I leaned over our daughter now I realized that some of the swelling had disappeared from her eyelids. When I spoke softly, her eyes partially opened, and my heart leaped with joy. "I'm so glad you're better, Darling.

41

You're getting well. Can you blink for me now? Try it. Blink your eyes, Honey.'' My pulse raced as her eyelids closed for an instant. *She does still have live brain cells; she can hear; she can respond.*

Several days later, on one of his rounds, the neurosurgeon asked, "If you can really get her to blink, show me."

The request was totally unexpected, and I sensed a note of challenge in his tone. Breathing a fervent prayer, I leaned over close to Sharon. "The doctor wants you to blink for us, Sharon. Please, Honey, blink your eyelids." Slowly but definitely they closed. "Blink them again, Dear." Again they closed. "Thank you, Darling. Can you blink them just once more?" Again her eyes closed.

I looked up and met the doctor's eyes. I will never forget his look. He turned, walked toward the door, then gazed back at me and said in his crisp, emphatic manner, "You've convinced me."

To this day, neither of us has mentioned the incident, but from then on I sensed an increased respect for my opinion regarding Sharon's care.

The difficult days slowly passed, their bleakness lighted by the warm compassion of relatives, friends and neighbors, expressed in varied ways. The food brought to the house was the finest—roasts, vegetables, salads, and desserts in abundance.

Harriet, my friend at the switchboard, gave me an electric coil that heated water in a cup, so I could make instant coffee in the room. Another friend brought a box of premoistened towelettes, so handy for keeping my hands clean. Another friend presented me with a Keepsake Edition of *Readers Digest* to read during the long hours.

Another close friend gave me a mustard seed pin, and told me: "My sister gave me one like this when our son had open-heart surgery. It served as a constant reminder of the power of faith, and helped me through many rough moments." Many times I felt deeply grateful for the reminder.

For several days Eileen wrote in her diary: "You are the same today." Then on Wednesday, November 22, the day before Thanksgiving, she wrote: "Well, I don't have to say you're the same, because you're better. I talked to you tonight and you opened your eyes real wide. You seemed like you are almost ready to wake up."

Thanksgiving Day I left the hospital for the first time, to eat dinner at my sister's. She had spent much time and energy in preparing a delicious meal, setting a beautiful table, and creating a cheery atmosphere with lovely flowers. I appreciated her thoughtfulness and enjoyed the meal and the atmosphere, yet I felt uneasy every moment, and was anxious to return to Sharon's bedside.

When the neurosurgeon came in the next day he spoke the words I'd been waiting two weeks to hear: "Well, it looks like she has a pretty good chance of making it now." But something in his tone and manner puzzled me.

Then the shocked thought came: Instead of being pleased, he sounds almost apologetic. Fear made speech difficult, but something stronger than fear controlled me as I replied, "I think I know what you are trying to tell me—that you hope it will be the right kind of living."

"Yes, her brain took a terrific beating; we don't know what to expect."

"She's going to be all right," I said emphatically. I firmly believed that.

Now a new development caused much anguish for us. Sharon seemed to be feeling pain, and she often moaned a great deal. One Sunday Eileen wrote: "Your dad can't stand to hear you cry like you do, and I don't think your mom can stand much more. However, she has gone through quite a bit."

Charley insisted I get away from the hospital, so my sister and two friends took turns staying for an hour or two while I went through the stores in the shopping center across the street.

Gay Christmas decorations hung everywhere, and a holiday spirit prevailed among the clerks and shoppers, but it seemed out of keeping with my mood. Each time I felt glad to return to Sharon's bedside.

The moaning changed to a wail—a pitiful, frightening sound. Then gradually, over the period of two or three days, it subsided. Her left hand now often fingered the feeding tube that protruded from her nose, but her right hand still didn't move.

One evening I glanced up to see Lynda and Eileen come into the room. I watched Sharon and thought, I'm sure her eyes are following them.

As they neared the bed Lynda said, "Hi, Sharon." The corners of Sharon's mouth moved, and a faint smile transformed her blank expression.

I can find no words to describe the thrill of that moment. The first smile of each of our three babies brought pleasure and excitement, but this smile stood alone in its importance. Her face was not paralyzed anymore; she could smile. She was aware of her friends. She could respond to them. I felt certain she would say, "Hi, Mom, what am I doing here?" any day now, and the long nightmare would be over. My whole being throbbed with a prayer of thanksgiving.

The last day of November the neurosurgeon informed me: "I am planning an extended vacation during the holiday season. I will be gone several weeks, so I think it best to remove the feeding tube before I leave. Its prolonged use often causes undesirable side effects, including extreme irritation. I feel sure she can be spoon fed now."

"That's fine with me." I smiled inwardly at this indication of progress.

The nurses reacted differently, with such remarks as: "We don't know if she can swallow. She may choke." They made no effort to keep their words out of Sharon's hearing, and I had the disturbing feeling that she knew what they were saying.

The neurosurgeon compromised, leaving orders for the nurses to supplement the tube feeding with mouth feeding for two days. He would then remove the tube if all went well.

I watched that first time, and while the nurse lifted a spoonful of cereal to Sharon's lips, I silently prayed, "Oh, please, dear God, let her swallow it." She opened her mouth and took the spoonful of food, then mouthed it for what seemed a very long time. Then she looked at me and I coaxed, "Swallow it, Honey, please swallow it." My breath caught as the moments passed; then I saw her throat muscles move, and the feeding tube danced up and down as she swallowed.

I glanced at the nurse, totally unprepared for the frown that greeted me as she snapped, "Well, she swallowed it, but you don't know when she may choke." Her thin fingers tightened around the spoon, she refilled it, and jabbed it toward Sharon's mouth.

Anger, dismay, and anguish swept over me. My daughter's pleading eyes looked straight into mine and the sickening realization struck me: She understands what the nurse said. Her lips trembled as the spoon touched them. Now my eyes pleaded but I remained silent. After a long, agonizing moment she swallowed again.

Later that day I watched her left hand move toward the feeding tube. She often fingered it, but suddenly I realized, by the deliberate way she yanked at it, that she intended to pull it out. The next day when the neurosurgeon came, I told him, "Sharon is expecting you to take the tube out today."

"Do you really think she understands enough to be expecting me to take it out?"

"Yes, I do."

He turned to Sharon, and with one quick movement the tube was out.

A full broad smile covered Sharon's face as she looked him straight in the eyes, plainly expressing her thanks.

He smiled back before leaving the room.

That day, December 1, Eileen wrote: "Today they took your tube out of your nose. You seem so much happier. Your mom seems happier too because you are." On December 7 she wrote: "I saw you last night, and what an improvement! You had chicken for dinner, and you seemed to enjoy it. You smiled for me. It sure made me feel good."

Our happiness was short-lived, however, for a few days later Sharon started vomiting. A stomach flu epidemic had been prevalent in our area. Some schools had been closed,

46

and many people were absent from their jobs. The vomiting brought a violent reaction from Sharon. She refused food and resisted all efforts to force her to eat.

Then I began to ache all over, and realized with a sense of panic that I had the flu. I had no choice but to go home to bed. For four days I remained home, miserable in mind and body, tortured every waking minute by the uncertainty of what was happening to Sharon. For over a month I had remained at the hospital night and day, but now when she needed me most of all I couldn't be there. I kept thinking over and over, if only her neurosurgeon were here.

When I finally returned to the hospital, a large "No Visitors" sign greeted me on the door. I entered the room and a cry of anguish caught in my throat. The girl who had been smiling only a few days before now stared at me with a wild look from eyes that appeared huge in the deathly pale face and emaciated body. A bottle hung at each side of the bed, and the tubing from them disappeared under the bedclothes. I pulled the blankets back to reveal painful-looking needles that carried fluid into Sharon's thighs. The nurse's explanation that this method had been resorted to because her veins were too small to use the regular IV method, and that Sharon did not feel pain because of the brain injury, did little to ease my mind. Her terrified screams when anyone came near proved that wrong, in my opinion.

There were other sounds in the air, though, that helped to ease my anguish—the sounds of Christmas. Upon our insistence, the "No Visitors" sign was removed and the door opened. I watched intently as carolers sang in the hall, hoping for a sign that Sharon was aware of them.

In my Christmas letter, which a friend dittoed for me, I told friends and relatives:

Christmas observance at the Gardners' will be different this year. There will be little frenzied preparation, and a minimum of shopping and gift-wrapping.

But the message of divine love and hope and faith comes to us with a deeper meaning and our hearts rejoice, perhaps as never before, as we hear the carols and the Scriptures, and wonder anew at the miracle of Christ's birth, life, and death for us. So our greeting, although the same old phrase, seems alive, vibrant and full of new meaning. Sharon's progress seems so slow to us, and at times we have felt that we have lost ground for days at a time. Perhaps that is God's special way of teaching us patience.

I desperately needed a giant portion of patience and faith to survive. A growing fear gnawed at me, as incident after incident caused me to question the quality of Sharon's care, even to the extent of wondering at times if she was being deliberately mistreated by one or more of the nurses.

One day the swing shift nurse told me that the doctor had remarked that someone was irritating Sharon, and he knew it wasn't her.

When an associate of the neurosurgeon changed the head bandage I was horrified to see a large nasty bump on Sharon's forehead. Upon questioning the nurses I was informed that she had fallen out of bed in the night.

I wondered why I hadn't heard about it before.

Sharon's lips were swollen and often bled, and her gums were very red. I wanted a specialist called in to see if anything could be done for them, and repeatedly called our family doctor's office, but could never reach him. I couldn't help but wonder if he was deliberately avoiding me, for day after weary day passed without my seeing him.

Finally, I made my request to the floor supervisor for a specialist to be consulted, but no action resulted.

I tried to convince Charley that I had a valid basis for my concern, but he felt I was simply overtired and over-wrought, and instead urged me to get away from the hospital more.

But no amount of urging could prevent me from spending every possible minute in Sharon's room. Intuition told me that she was in great danger, from what source, or of what nature I did not know (and still don't) but to me then, and even as I look back on it today, the danger was very real and terrifying.

I rushed back from meal breaks and stayed as late as possible in the evenings, although at Charley's insistence I did go home to sleep. I no longer visited with friends for long periods in the lobby or in the hall. My place was by Sharon's bedside.

Often the mustard seed pin brought me back from despondence with the realization that "with God all things are possible," and the reminder that I could depend on God's promises. He would bring victory even in the desperate situation we now faced, for He had promised that our daughter would be all right. This knowledge constantly kept the ray of hope burning.

Our pastor, Rev. John Nastari, made regular visits to the hospital, and the comfort and encouragement of his presence and his well-chosen words helped to keep me from giving up. I remember on one of his visits I told him: "I know that Sharon is going to be all right, for God has promised it, but I keep wondering if I am doing all that I can. Am I carrying out my full responsibility?"

His expression of tender compassion said even more than his words: "You're doing all that is humanly possible. Rest assured God knows that, and doesn't expect more, and you shouldn't expect more of yourself, either."

Two other faithful visitors whose quiet presence spoke volumes were Jeanne Chancellor, a school friend of Sharon's, and her mother. Each day they came—sometimes tiptoeing into the room, sometimes just standing for a few minutes at the door; but always a special blessing came with them.

One evening a surprised doctor found me there when he came into the room at a very late hour. He assured me that the painful needle-feeding method would be abandoned in the next day or two, and the feeding tube replaced.

He listened intently while I told him, "Things aren't right. I'm convinced that Sharon is not getting proper care. In fact I'm fearful that she is being deliberately mistreated. I've tried to get a chance to talk to you about it for a long time. I'd like to have the day nurse replaced."

He made no comment or promise. On December 20, he fired the nurse on duty from 11 p.m. to 7 a.m., but the day nurse remained.

With the needles removed, my hopes again mounted.

The wild, terrified look eased, and she seemed relaxed and calm, but unresponsive. The nourishment from the tube feeding will soon have her smiling and aware again, I told myself. It will just take a little time.

Despite a busy Christmas schedule, dear Eileen still popped in occasionally. Together we decorated a little Christmas tree for Sharon, putting on tinsel and ornaments until the branches drooped from their weight. Then I wrapped gifts and placed them underneath, daring to let myself believe that our Sharon would open them on Christmas Day.

The day nurse had requested Christmas Day off. I felt pleased when a nurse on the regular staff of the hospital agreed to replace her, for she had always shown a special interest in our daughter and I felt she would try hard to get response from Sharon.

"Give her one of her gifts as soon as you come on duty," I told her. "She always opens her presents the first thing on Christmas morning."

5

No Rock Too Huge

ON CHRISTMAS DAY I WENT TO THE HOSPITAL, determined to try hard to keep a resolution I had just made that I would put out of my mind any thoughts about irregularities in Sharon's care. I thought that perhaps my fears were unfounded. Anyway, I couldn't do anything about it, and my dwelling on it was driving me to the brink of a nervous breakdown. And now Christmas had come without fulfilling my hopes. I recalled with a sharp pang Sharon's vacant stare when her unopened gift fell to the floor a short while before.

During the next few days, many other things tore at me. Why couldn't something be done about Sharon's painful-looking gums and lips? Her arms and legs were kept tied to the bed much of the time now, and she strained hard to get them loose. It was pitiful to watch her. The nurses insisted they had to restrain her, as she resisted medical attention, and often tried to pull at the feeding tube. I felt sure that if the neurosurgeon were there many changes would be made.

The floor supervisor had told me that I had to leave the room when she was receiving treatment. Often I heard her screams where I waited at the end of the hall. I begged Charley to either let me bring her home or take her to another hospital, but he considered the idea ridiculous. I felt his increasing concern for me.

One afternoon he insisted I go for a long ride, quieting my protests with an emphatic assurance: "The fresh air and sunshine will be good for you." My reaction must have hurt him deeply, for I remained stony silent, letting fear and anguish eat at me until I burst out, "If anything happens to Sharon, I'll never forgive you for not letting me get her away from that hospital." Fear controlled my thinking to such an extent that it had temporarily crowded out God's definite assurance that Sharon would be all right. How foolish to let myself believe for even a moment that any human force could prevent the fulfillment of one of God's promises.

I once again clung desperately to that promise during the next week, for Sharon's condition worsened and her fever raged. On the morning of January 3 I found an "Isolation" sign on her closed door. The floor supervisor informed me that Sharon had a staph infection, and that anyone entering the room must wear a hospital uniform over their clothes and leave it in the room when they departed.

My hands trembled as I put on a uniform. I entered the room and a muffled groan escaped me. The pale thin form on the bed lay deadly still, no restlessness now. Her body, ravaged by infection and fever, appeared lifeless.

54

One ray of hope came as I realized her neurosurgeon would be back in just two days. Fervently I prayed, "O God, please give me strength, and help her to hang on until he returns."

In midmorning the door burst open, and the doctor stood there. He was back two days early from vacation. I stared at him in wonder at the way God answers prayer.

The doctor's expression and manner showed shocked consternation as he examined Sharon and gave curt instructions to the nurse.

My memory blurs as I try to recall details of those next few days. I remember going across to the shopping center to telephone the doctor, and unloading some of my misgiving and anxiety. I told him I was no longer allowed in the room during treatment, and he quickly assured me, "Well, I don't run the hospital, but I'll certainly try to get that changed."

The next morning when I walked into the room, instead of the nurse with the wrinkled face and long thin fingers, a young woman with a cheerful smile and competent manner greeted me. The neurosurgeon had ordered the replacement, and also arranged with the hospital that I was to be allowed in the room at any time.

Together with the nurses I struggled to keep Sharon alive, control her fever, and stem the infection. Three days later her fever broke. Another crisis had passed.

Gradually she began to "emerge"—to follow movements with her eyes, to cuddle her head against me and smile when I hugged her, and to hold an object we handed her. I noticed with joy and relief that she could now move her right arm in an awkward manner, without bending her wrist or moving her fingers.

55

Other actions puzzled and disturbed me. Sharon kicked her legs high in the air, so it was difficult to keep even a sheet over them. She babbled a good deal, and I tried hard to make sense out of the unintelligible sounds. Her dad handed her watch to her one day and she played with it a few seconds, then dropped it over the side of the bed. The nurse gave her a magazine and she stared at it a few moments, upside down.

I don't know when the realization finally came that her actions were those of an infant, and that she was indeed an infant in all respects except physical development. I must have subconsciously known it a long time before it registered fully on my conscious mind. The shock of the realization, combined with the strain of the long weeks now resulted in my often experiencing confused thinking. I wondered if it was apparent to others. On one occasion I noticed my sister in earnest conversation with the doctor, out of my hearing, and another time Charley walked far down the hall talking to him. Then one afternoon the neurosurgeon informed me gently but firmly that I was not to come to the hospital for several days.

I paced the floor at home, unable to make myself perform any of the household tasks that needed doing. I was away from the hospital physically, but not mentally, and I simply could not cope with the resulting tension.

I didn't even argue with Charley's suggestion that I go to a hospital as a patient for a few days, so he made the necessary arrangements with the neurosurgeon and I was admitted to another hospital in our area.

The first two days and nights were one long nightmare of imaginings, of restless wakefulness, of inner struggle. I've always detested tranquilizers or sleeping pills, so instead of letting the nurses know I was awake through the night, I feigned sleep whenever they came into the room. Then at last when I realized my utter helplessness and my inability to heal myself, I finally leaned back on God's arms and rested. Oh, the blessed peace and relief of those hours and days! I silently quoted passage after passage of Scripture, beloved Psalms, parts of the Gospels and Paul's letters, along with poetry memorized long before. Lines and music from cherished hymns echoed in my mind. Sometimes I sang them softly in the bathroom I used across the hall. One day I emerged to find the neurosurgeon waiting with the nurse outside the door for me. She told me later he had been concerned when he found me missing from my room. I wondered if he heard my singing.

I now know that during those days that renewed my strength and my faith, my husband and my son experienced one of the most difficult times of their lives.

The pressures of Charley's job in addition to his home duties and the newly assumed responsibility of two hospital patients weighed heavily on him.

Les, already grief-stricken over his twin, bore the added burden of anxiety for me. His world had fallen apart and his schoolwork suffered; some of his grades reached rock bottom. This deeply disturbed Charley, and he was also disturbed by the latest problems with Sharon.

The feeding tube had been removed again, and the nurses struggled to get Sharon to eat, without success. She drank water, but refused anything else. Then one Sunday when her neurosurgeon was in another town performing emergency surgery, she had a convulsion. They called Charley to come to the hospital immediately, evidently believing death was imminent. For several hours doctors worked over her while Charley watched. He told me later, "I can't describe the agony I felt as I waited and prayed. Your words: 'If anything happens to Sharon I'll never forgive you,' kept going through my mind."

My frenzied outburst had placed a tremendous additional burden on his already overloaded shoulders. When finally the doctors pronounced her out of danger, Charley was near collapse from the strain.

I remained blissfully unaware of the latest crisis until after I returned home. For some reason that I didn't understand, but had come to accept, God had removed from me the responsibility for my daughter's welfare, and He alone was in charge. With thanksgiving and relief I recalled the truth I had learned five years before from Sharon's first accident, that no matter how helpless I am in caring for my loved ones, there is no limit to the power of my loving God.

I feel a deep sense of awe now as I think how the five days of hospitalization prepared me, as perhaps nothing else could have, for the years ahead. It provided the spiritual renewal and the physical rest I needed.

I returned home the morning of January 17. When Les arrived from school that afternoon, his excitement at finding me home and his eagerness to do things for me brought a twinge of guilt as I realized how little attention I'd given him the last two months, at a time when he desperately needed it. I hoped I could make it up to him. I worked, a little at a time, between hospital visits, trying to make our house a home once again.

At the hospital the struggle to persuade Sharon to eat continued, without success. Our hopes grew, however, at the progress in other areas. She could now say "nurse," and did so loudly and frequently; she could walk with assistance; and sometimes she used the bedpan or toilet. We took her wallet to her, with pictures of her schoolmates, and she sat for long periods flipping them back and forth, looking at them.

We put a radio in her room and at times the music seemed to calm her, to bring a measure of relief from her restlessness.

The continuing efforts to force her to eat, however, caused her to resist wildly whenever anyone approached her for anything. We asked our church and many of our other friends to pray with us that a solution might be found, for she couldn't continue to live much longer without food. We faced what appeared to be an impassable obstacle, yet God's promise remained sure. With certainty I knew:

No rock too huge, nor wall too steep
for God to move or faith to leap.

6

Sharon's Homecoming

MONDAY MORNING, JANUARY 22, 1962, the telephone rang just after Les had left for school. When I answered I heard the voice of Sharon's day nurse, and my heart started pounding.

"Is this Mrs. Gardner?"

"Yes, it is."

"Sharon's neurosurgeon thinks she would be better off at home. How soon can you come for her?"

The kaleidoscope of thoughts that whizzed through my mind, and my dry mouth made speech difficult, but after a moment I managed to reply, "We'll come for her in an hour."

I hung up while the full impact of what I had just said flooded over me. What would Charley say? I really had no choice, I reasoned. She hadn't said, "Will you come for her?" but, "How soon can you come for her?" I recognized a tone of urgency in her voice.

61

"O dear God, help me say the right thing to convince Charley."

Then he was in the room asking, "Who called?"

"The day nurse. She said the neurosurgeon thinks Sharon would be better off at home and wanted to know how soon we could come for her. I told her we'd be there in about an hour."

"You what?" He fairly shouted the words. "How in the world do you think you can handle her at home?"

I looked at Charley, standing now in stunned silence, and tried to imagine the thoughts going through his mind. It had only been four days since he had brought me home from the hospital, and he had good reason to wonder if I would be able to cope with all the responsibility of handling Sharon at home. I realized then that God had prepared me in a special way through those days in the hospital. I needed the rest, but even more I needed the close fellowship with God they provided. But Charley hadn't had any rest. Instead, he had been loaded down with increased responsibilities.

His next question interrupted my thoughts. "Do you really think you can do more for Sharon than three round-the-clock nurses and all the hospital equipment?"

"No, Dear, I don't think I can. But I do think that love can, the kind of love we will show to her at home. I feel we can calm her fears, and get her to eat again. Evidently her doctor thinks so too."

"But what about you? You'll break completely under the strain."

"The worst strain for me is not being able to be with Sharon all the time, and not to know what's happening. The physical responsibility will be greater, but there will be less mental stress. Can't we at least try it and see if we can get her to eat?''

Another long silence ensued, and in the stillness I asked God for guidance. When Charley finally spoke, his tone conveyed his reluctance, but my heart sang with thanksgiving at his words: "OK. You get her room ready while I go after gas and stop by the office."

The sun shone brightly and I opened the windows of Sharon's room to let in the fresh, crisp air while I hurriedly vacuumed, dusted, and rearranged the room so it would be easy to get Sharon in and out of bed. It needed a thorough cleaning, but that would have to wait.

We spoke little on the way; I felt breathless from excitement and apprehension. When we arrived at the hospital, I went on up to room 300 while Charley went to the business office.

Sharon was sitting up and stared at me wide-eyed when I came in. I picked up her bathrobe and started to put it on her. Her arms stiffened, she hugged them close to her body and pulled away from me with a look of wild terror.

I talked to her gently while I tried again. "I just want to put your bathrobe on you, Honey. I'm not going to hurt you." But still she fought, resisting with a strength that amazed me.

I didn't realize that Charley had come into the room and had been watching our struggle until he exploded, "How in the world do you think you can handle her at home?"

For a moment Sharon sat motionless, then her whole body shook with sobs. My eyes met Charley's, and my heart leaped, for I saw a flicker of hope. The awe in his voice, and his soft-spoken words confirmed it, "She understood what I said."

We finally got the bathrobe on Sharon and took her downstairs to the car. Charley had the car at the emergency entrance by the time the nurse and I arrived with the wheelchair and its occupant. When we opened the door for Sharon she took hold of the handle and pulled herself toward the seat. She needed little help to get in. The nurse looked at me and smiled. "She's ready to go home."

We half led and half carried her into the house and to her bedroom. As we helped her into bed, she panted from exhaustion.

My breath came quickly too, partly from exertion and partly from the full realization of my inadequacy for the responsibility I now faced. I had no medical advice to follow, no instructions, nor any training or experience to fit me for my task. My only qualifications were a deep love for the patient, an abiding faith in her recovery, and the assurance of God's guidance.

I expected Charley to leave for work right away, and was relieved when he said he'd stay in case I needed him.

We attempted to get Sharon to drink some milk, talking softly to her as we struggled to force the liquid through her tightly closed lips. Then we tried pineapple juice, orange juice and grape juice; but her resistance increased with each try, and the wild terrified look returned. Finally we offered her water and she drank it.

Later Charley suggested we try forcing milk into her mouth with a syringe. He thought if we could get her to swallow some, maybe we could conquer her fear.

We waited until Les came home from school; then he and his dad applied the only kind of restraints we ever used, loving hands and arms. While I tried to force the milk between her locked teeth, I talked to her. "We just want you to drink some milk, Sharon. We love you and wouldn't do anything to hurt you. Please open your mouth."

But it remained tightly closed. Finally I succeeded in forcing the syringe between her teeth, and squeezed some milk into her mouth. It ran back out. We were getting nowhere! Once again I squeezed the syringe, while I held her lips together with my other hand. Some of the milk dripped out the sides of her mouth, but I held on. Finally her throat muscles moved as she swallowed.

We tried the same procedure several more times during the late afternoon and evening with minimal success. Our efforts had forced her to swallow some of the milk, but we had a long way to go to conquer her fear.

When bedtime came we wondered how we'd manage during the night. Our room and Sharon's faced each other, with a short hallway between. We left both doors open so we could hear her, and sank exhausted into bed.

Evidently all the exertion had exhausted Sharon too, for she slept right through the night.

As I watched Charley and Les leave the next morning, the responsibility of everything that lay before me weighed on my mind. I realized I dared not move one inch on my own and I began that day to experience a new dimension in faith and trust. I felt the same calm assurance I remembered as a small child when one of my parents held my hand when we walked an unfamiliar road.

I relied heavily on that inner assurance through that difficult morning. When I tried to bathe and change Sharon and put clean sheets on her soaked bed, she fought wildly, her eyes wide with fear. I coaxed and tugged, and finally succeeded in getting the bed changed and a clean gown on her, but she seemed so terrified when I tried to bathe her that I finally gave up, after having washed only her face and hands.

When I attempted to get her to drink a glass of milk, I met the same terrified resistance, accompanied by a loud "no," one of the few words that now made up her vocabulary.

She used another word many times that morning, "nurse, nurse." Once when she called loudly I put her on the bedpan and she used it. I felt encouraged by this sign of progress, and praised her for it.

I offered her fruit juices several times, which she refused; but when I brought water to her she drank it. I left the empty glass by her bed, and once when she called "nurse" she held it out to me. I refilled it with water and she drank it rapidly.

Charley came home early that afternoon. I hated to answer his eager question, "Did you get her to drink anything today?" We both knew we couldn't keep her home unless we could get her to take nourishment.

Then Charley had another idea. "If she insists on drinking only water, that's how she's going to have to get her nourishment. So why not try Karo in the next glass?" We put a teaspoonful in the next water we offered her, and she drank it.

When Les came home we again forced milk into her mouth with a syringe. When she finally swallowed it, Les told her, "See, that didn't hurt you. It tastes good, doesn't it?" She seemed to swallow the next syringe full with less struggle, and I dared to hope we had finally made some progress.

That night I made the first entry in a notebook I started keeping to record her daily intake.

She began to drink the milk from a glass a few sips at a time throughout the day, sometimes only after a great deal of urging, but she seemed less frightened.

Friday's record included two separate entries: "1/3 graham cracker," "1/2 graham cracker." Both Charley and I vividly recall the expression on her face when she took the first bite, and the questioning manner in which she held it in her mouth, then finally chewed it slowly and swallowed it.

Another notation on that day's record marked another milestone: "Moved to front room." From then on she started sitting in the living room for several hours a day.

She drank 24 ounces of milk that Friday with 12 teaspoons Meritine, a food supplement. The increase was accomplished only with a great deal of patient effort, except for one instance that evening when my impatient reaction achieved surprising results.

Les had offered to give Sharon a glass of milk. I watched as he held the glass out to her.

"Here's some milk for you, Sharon."

She looked at him defiantly. "No."

"Come on, drink it—it's good for you."

His voice pleaded, but her expression didn't change. Then, with a quick movement, she knocked the glass out of his hand, and the milk splattered over the rug.

Les stood staring at his twin with a hurt look of dismay. Before I quite realized what I was doing, my arm shot out and I slapped Sharon's cheek as I told her, "We all love you and are trying to do all we can for you, Sharon, but we won't allow you to act like that."

67

I went to the kitchen, refilled the glass, then held it out to her with a stern command, "Drink this." We stared at each other for a moment, then she took the glass and drank all the milk.

With the incident came the realization that discipline would have to be a vital part of our care for Sharon. Just as our three babies had soon learned that unacceptable behavior brought quick punishment, so must Sharon.

The responsibility weighed heavily on me that night as I lay in bed, too disturbed for sleep, and I prayed again, "God, teach me patience and give me wisdom."

7

Progress

THE LONG DIFFICULT HOURS of each day now included many thrilling moments as we saw one indication after another that love was beginning to conquer Sharon's fear.

We no longer had to coax her to drink milk. Often after emptying one eight-ounce glass she would hold it out for a refill.

On her tenth day home we recorded a total consumption of more than two quarts of milk, fortified with food supplement and an egg, plus 16 graham crackers. At last her starved body was receiving nourishment. I had hopes that healthy flesh would soon cover the bones that now protruded.

That afternoon I coaxed her to stand on the bathroom scales. Dressed in pajamas, bathrobe, and slippers, she weighed 105 pounds. Before the accident she had weighed 130, which seemed about right for her large frame and five-foot-seven-inch height.

The next day, at Charley's suggestion, I put some dry cereals on a TV tray by her bed. She picked up a few, smelled them, played with them for a while, finally put one in her mouth, then another and another, until the tray was empty. For several weeks I refilled the tray many times a day.

Our neighbor, Trudy Carlson, rolled together tiny portions of bread and ham to resemble puffed rice, and we placed them on the tray. She ate them along with the cereals.

I discontinued the intake record after three weeks. It no longer seemed necessary. Then I started noting on paper exciting firsts in our child's development. One evening when I helped Sharon into her bedroom during her fourth week home she turned on the light switch when we entered the room. As light flooded the room, joy filled my heart.

A few days later the extension phone in her room rang when I stood by her bed. Before I could reach it, she lifted the receiver and answered a soft "Hello." She held it to her ear for a few moments, then told the caller: "She wants to speak to you now," and handed the phone to me.

My emotion-filled voice sounded so unnatural that Rickey, on the other end of the line, asked: "What's wrong, Grandma? Are you crying?"

I assured him that there was nothing wrong, but didn't answer his last question. How could I explain to a four-year-old that I cried because of extreme happiness?

Sharon now used the bathroom regularly during the day. Like any normal, inquisitive child, she delighted in opening the boxes of powder, bobby pins and tissue, and tearing off long streamers of toilet paper. Also like a normal child, she started watching television.

Her stack of get-well cards increased with each day's mail, and one morning I handed her three new arrivals. She opened each one, looked at the cards, and replaced them in the envelopes. What fun she'll have someday reading them all, I thought. How soon that would be I couldn't guess, but I felt certain that the time would come.

I made an appointment with Sharon's neurosurgeon, and looked forward to his comments with eager anticipation as I contrasted in my mind our happy inquisitive child with the terrified creature Sharon had been when he last saw her.

A long-time friend drove us to the appointment. During the ride Sharon delighted us with her excited exclamations, and we shared her joy as she saw, for the first time in her memory, beauty that we considered commonplace. When we entered the doctor's waiting room, I noticed with relief that no one else was waiting.

Sharon didn't want to sit down; instead she walked around the room, looking at the furnishings. Then an ashtray caught her eye, and before I could rescue it, ashes covered her fingers.

While the nurse dressed Sharon after the examination, I sat in the doctor's conference room and related in glowing terms many examples of Sharon's progress during the seven weeks she had been home. Then I waited for his comments, confident that he must now be convinced that she would be all right; that she would return to near-normal.

The doctor stared across the desk at me for a moment, then in his crisp professional tone said, "Well, she has made some progress; she appears to function in some areas at about a five-year level now. We don't know

71

how far she can advance, nor how long progress may continue. After all, her brain took a terrific beating.''

That was all, no pat on the back for us, no assurance for the future, no guidelines. I felt disappointment and discouragement tinged with anger.

That night, with the doctor's words echoing in my mind, I had difficulty falling asleep. Then other words, ''She's going to be all right,'' replaced the echo. ''Forgive me, God,'' I prayed, ''for again letting human evaluation dim Your promise.''

I awoke the next morning with the serene feeling that comes from refreshing sleep and the certain knowledge that God is close. For a few moments after my morning prayer, I lay still, thinking over the events of the last seven weeks. My crowded days left little time for thought. Many things about Sharon's behavior puzzled me, and I mulled them over, trying to put some of the pieces together in my mind.

Several incidents indicated to me that Sharon retained at least a vague memory of her family and friends. One day when Stella stopped by with the children, Sharon stared at baby Mike and inquired, ''Yours?'' When Stella told her that was her baby named Mike, Sharon frowned and shook her head: ''I don't remember.'' Since Mike had been less than six weeks old at the time of her accident, it seemed logical that she might have retained some memory of the rest of the family but not of him. Perhaps that was due to the fact that she had pictures of the rest of the Browns, but not of Mike.

Sharon's increasing vocabulary thrilled me, yet I couldn't understand why some phrases, even sentences, popped out clearly, yet try as I might I couldn't get her to repeat simple names of objects or to say words like milk, water, Mama.

I still responded to her insistent "nurse." But how I longed to hear her say "Mama" and know she had some idea of the meaning of the word.

She now seemed to want attention and affection from her brother and father. Sometimes she would snuggle up close to one of them on the couch, but she still often recoiled from my touch.

Then the simple explanation began to take shape in my mind. During the ten weeks of Sharon's hospital stay, I had been there so much of the time, helping the nurses care for her. And those uniforms I'd worn when she was in isolation! Why, of course, why hadn't I thought of it before? Sharon's confused mind considered me a part of the hospital, a nurse who had come home with her. No wonder she distrusted me! What could I do about it?

This question, like so many others, remained unanswered. I had little time or energy to seek answers. I rushed through each day, trying to accomplish the absolute essentials, but leaving so much undone. Everywhere I looked, dust and clutter threatened to overwhelm me.

It was then that a friend suggested we share a housekeeper. And so it was that Bessie came to work for us four hours a week. What a blessing she was! The clean house delighted Sharon, and so did the attention our new employee gave her. Soon the two became fast friends.

On one of Bessie's workdays I left the house a short time to grocery shop, and when I returned Bessie met me at the door, a distressed look on her face.

"The new divan that you had ordered came while you were gone. Sharon got so excited when she saw it, and

73

before I could stop her, or hardly realize what she was doing, she ran up to the deliveryman saying: 'Oh, thank you, thank you.' Then she threw her arms around him and kissed him. You can't imagine the look on that man's face. I didn't know what to say or do.''

I found myself in the same dilemma, not knowing what to say or do, many times. A child's inquisitive, impulsive mind housed in a teenager's active body, made a strange combination, difficult to cope with.

I became acutely aware of this one day when I took Sharon into a Woolworth store. She darted in and out of the counters, as if playing hide-and-seek. I chased after her, almost colliding with several persons as I ran. I'd gain on her and she'd look back at me and laugh, then take off again at a faster pace. Finally, panting from exhaustion, I captured her. Only then did I look up and see the astonished expression on the faces of several people who had evidently stopped to watch. Holding tightly to her arm, I quickly guided her out of the store, my face red from embarrassment. Now I can laugh about it.

Yet in addition to the difficulties, the strange combination of child-teenager provided a thrilling and exciting challenge. We constantly sought ways to improve her behavior, stimulate her thinking, and help her learn.

During our April visit to the neurosurgeon, I asked if it wasn't time to start Sharon on a regular educational program. He agreed that she could now benefit from schooling and suggested that we apply to our district for a home teacher.

We did, and for the remaining six weeks of the school term Mrs. Enderton came three times a week. With patience and amazing dedication she started Sharon on the road to formal education. She cheerfully accepted· the challenge of her strange, new assignment and her pupil's unpredictable behavior. Often she spent many hours of her own time in the evening poring over books about the brain.

She would write out words and have Sharon copy them in a notebook. Although Sharon didn't know what she was writing, she seemed to get the feel of the letters and copied them quite well. She also talked into the tape recorder, then listened in excitement as it repeated her words. She wrote numbers and began to count.

We bought preschool puzzles, and she spent many hours fitting them together. Les devised a method of game playing that helped his twin with arithmetic. He dealt two playing cards to her and two to himself and the one whose cards added up to the highest total took that hand. When she learned to add two cards easily, he increased the number to three, then to four, five and six. She enjoyed the game, and the attention from Les it provided, and soon she learned to add quite well.

I noted each accomplishment and watched eagerly for the next. I felt, however, that the medication Sharon had been taking ever since her return home made her lethargic at times and hindered her learning process. I experimented by gradually cutting down the dose, and by the date of our next visit to the neurosurgeon I had entirely eliminated it. "That's fine with me," he said. "If she starts having seizures we may have to put her back on it, but if she can get by without any she'll be better off." She never took another dose.

Each day now provided new thrills for us as her ability to learn increased and we explored new avenues for teaching. On weekends we took her for long rides, sharing her excitement and realizing anew the truth of her oft-repeated phrase, "Oh, the world is so beautiful."

Some of her school friends still visited, and shared our joy in her accomplishments. The fact that Sharon still called me "nurse" particularly concerned them, and I would often hear one of them coaxing her, "Say Mo-ther, please say Mo-ther." Then one day Lynda's excited voice reached me in the kitchen, "Mrs. Gardner, would you please come in here?" Three pairs of eyes watched as I entered Sharon's room, and then Lynda and Joanne looked at Sharon and Lynda prompted, "Say it now." A long moment passed, then a grin spread across Sharon's face, and she said slowly and plainly, "Mo-ther."

I hurriedly left the room, tears streaming from my eyes, just as they do now every time I recall that moment. That one word was payment, heaped up and running over, for all my efforts.

8

A School for Sharon

MRS. ENDERTON SUGGESTED we enroll Sharon in a six-week remedial reading course at San Jose State College. Since I don't drive, I took Sharon by bus, and during the 30 minutes enroute I wondered whether the course would be worth all the effort. But before we caught the bus home that day I realized that no other duty could be as important as bringing Sharon each day. Both Mrs. Keith, the teacher assigned to work individually with Sharon during the one hour pupil-teacher session, and Dr. Paul Betten, the department head, displayed enthusiasm and a determination to explore every possibility in meeting the unusual challenge of working with Sharon.

Each day for the entire six weeks Dr. Betten conferred with Mrs. Keith and they discussed the effectiveness of the period just ended; then they planned for the next day. Sharon displayed ability and eagerness to learn, and before the course ended she had learned her ABC's and sounds and could read some simple words.

She also attended a speech clinic three afternoons a week during the six-week period.

I benefited, as well, for I brought along library books on the subject of the brain and brain damage. During the hours when I sat and waited for Sharon, I studied, and gained needed insight.

The week after summer school ended, I telephoned our school district office for an appointment regarding Sharon's placement for the fall semester. I looked forward to the opportunity of reporting on her progress during the summer and planning for the coming school year. I intended to request a home teacher, and also to ask that Sharon be allowed to attend one class at her own high school to retain contact with her peers.

The appointment, however, turned out to be a discouraging one. We were quickly told by a businesslike woman that the district doesn't furnish home teachers when a pupil is able to leave home. Then, after a 15-minute interview with Sharon she told me that their decision was to assign Sharon to the continuation school for that year.

"Have you considered what effect that environment might have on Sharon?" I asked. I couldn't believe that she really intended to place her in the "problem" school of the district, filled with parolees, expellees, and pregnant girls. "And what about transportation? How will she get there?"

"That's up to you. The school doesn't furnish transportation. She doesn't have to go to school, you know. Judging by the test I just gave her, I doubt that she will be able to profit much from schooling, anyway."

I left her office in a state of shocked disbelief, bitter

protests raging in my mind. All the arguments I should have presented in verbal rebuttal went through my mind now. Sharon had been an honor-roll student, well liked by her teachers and peers. She had been an enthusiastic participant in a wide variety of school activities, and had supported student responsibility at every opportunity. For her to be brushed aside like this just because she had suffered severe injury was gross injustice.

If she had been physically injured, no matter to what degree, she would have received adequate educational help. Why should it be denied her because the damage had been to her brain? One of Sharon's greatest needs, I thought, is for companionship with those of her peers who can show her, by their example, proper behavior. What will association with this group of students do to her?

During the weeks remaining before the school term I struggled with these and other similar questions, but came up with no answers. I realized I could not expect to find a classroom that would adequately fit Sharon's unique needs.

I held on to the hope that an application we had placed with the Stanford Speech Clinic would be accepted, and that she could start therapy soon, but that wouldn't take the place of regular schooling, only supplement it.

Finally we decided to enroll her in the continuation school, but to keep searching for a better placement.

We soon realized that the school had some distinct educational advantages. A maximum of 50 pupils comprised the student body, and the highly qualified teachers showed a special concern for each of them. Because of the small classes, each pupil received much individual instruction.

79

Early in October, however, an incident occurred which strengthened our conviction that the placement was not right for our daughter.

Sharon arrived home from school that October day noticeably upset.

"Did you know that nearly all of the kids at my school have been ex...ex..."

"Expelled?"

"They think I've been ex...expelled, too."

Her voice conveyed her anguish at the shocking fact she had just learned, and at the realization that she was so classified.

"Why can't I go back to Lincoln with all my friends?" Her lips quivered, and her eyes mirrored all the hurt and longing stored up within her. I shared her frustration, and felt that I must make every effort to find other schooling for her.

We learned of a tutor, experienced in working with brain-damaged persons, who lived in Palo Alto, some 20 miles away. I contacted her and made arrangements for private tutoring. I would take Sharon by bus twice a week for an hour's lesson. One afternoon it started raining while we were enroute. When we got off the bus Sharon refused to get under my umbrella. Instead she walked in the rain, holding her face up so the drops would fall on it. Excitement was evident in her voice as she exclaimed, "Oh, it feels so good, Mama! I love it!"

Then I realized this was her first experience of feeling rain. I vividly recalled the first time she looked out of the window and saw rain. She had called me excitedly.

"Mama, Mama, water! It's falling from the sky!"

When we reached the tutor's home, Sharon hesitated

outside; "Do you think it will still be raining when we go home?" she asked.

"Yes, I think it will."

"I sure hope so."

I doubt if she learned much from her books that day, but her thrilling experience with one of nature's wonders made the trip worthwhile.

Often firsthand experiences proved to be the best teaching medium, not only for Sharon, but for all of us.

One weekend we took her to Santa Cruz, a pleasant ocean resort town with a large beach area, about 30 miles from us. Since early childhood our children have enjoyed going there.

Sharon ran up and down the beach, laughing, throwing sand, watching the rolling waves and letting the cold water cover her feet. We had to keep constant watch and repeatedly insist she move back from the high waves. We told her she had been there many times before, but she shook her head with a haunted look, trying so hard to recall the past.

"I don't remember ever seeing this place before," she said.

I kept hoping some incident, some remembered place or familiar face would provide a link to the past. I had heard of instances where persons with severe amnesia had suddenly "woken up" and I kept secretly hoping Sharon would too; that someday memory would return, and the long nightmare would be over.

One evening Charley was showing some of our home slides. Among them was a picture of Sharon taken before the accident. She let out an excited exclamation, "Me! Me!" then ran up to the screen and patted her long hair.

81

Many times she had indicated by her actions that she disliked her short hair, not yet grown out since her head had been shaved in the hospital.

Another time she remarked, "I didn't think I'd ever been anywhere but here."

Early in November the letter I had been waiting for arrived. We had an appointment for an evaluation at the Stanford speech clinic on November 8. I looked forward to the date, confident the clinic could help Sharon.

I watched, intrigued, during the evaluation session from an adjoining room, through a one-way window. On Sharon's side the window was a mirror, so she was unaware that I could see her.

The therapist took several objects out of a box: two pencils, a small bell, a cup, a spoon, a lock, and a key. Then she told Sharon, "Pick up one of the pencils and then ring the bell."

Sharon picked up one of the pencils, but seemed confused about the bell, and mumbled something about a school bell. Finally she picked it up and smiled as it started to tinkle.

Her therapist smiled back and said, "That's right, Sharon. Now pick up the key."

She looked from one object to another, with a bewildered expression.

"Can you place the bell between the pencil and the spoon?"

Sharon picked up the bell and placed it between the two pencils.

"Now put the spoon in the cup."

She put the pencil in the cup.

"Close the lock, please."

Sharon hesitated a long moment, then slowly reached for the lock and closed it.

"Do you know what a robin is?" the therapist asked Sharon.

"I know a girl named Robin."

Her reply surprised me. She hadn't seen Robin for a long time, certainly not since her accident. Why should she remember her? Then I recalled the picture of Robin among her snapshots. Was this the reason she had retained the memory?

The therapist pointed outside the window.

"Do you know what the robins are that are out there?"

Sharon looked puzzled and shook her head.

"Robins are birds, Sharon."

"I know what a bird is. I like birds."

The therapist handed Sharon some paper and then showed her a card. "Copy on the paper the letters on this card."

Some were capital letters, some small. Sharon copied them all as small letters.

She has the same problem with teaspoons and tablespoons when she sets the table for me, I thought. She doesn't seem to be able to distinguish the difference in size.

The therapist instructed Sharon to repeat a sentence after her, and she repeated the few words well. She became quite confused, however, when she was asked to repeat longer sentences.

"Draw a man on this paper, Sharon."

The man's arms came out from his waist.

The therapist instructed Sharon to manipulate her tongue in various ways, and she did this well. She then

83

pronounced a list of words and asked Sharon to point to each of them on a card. Sharon pointed to all of them correctly.

After the test I had a short conference with the therapist. She expressed surprise at the rapidity of Sharon's speech. "Usually after such an injury speech is slow and labored," she said. "In contrast, Sharon's speech is rapid, but not distinct, which makes it difficult for her to be understood. We will try to help her in that respect, as well as in speech comprehension."

I went home that day with another book to study, a small one on understanding aphasia. In the letter Sharon's neurosurgeon had written to the clinic he had mentioned that she had severe aphasia. The term was just another unfamiliar word to me. The booklet explained that it means "loss of language," and gave suggestions on how to help the patient.

I also felt thankful for the opportunity the speech therapy would afford. I had made arrangements for private sessions three times a week.

"I can't wait to tell Les that I'm going to be taking lessons at Stanford," Sharon said and her eyes sparkled with excitement.

Les provided an essential service for Sharon now, that of listener. She told him in minute detail what happened at school and how she felt about not being allowed to go to Lincoln. She also poured out a variety of hurts, frustrations, and disappointments. Often she would ask, "What would you do, Les?" Having a twin to share all her sorrows and happiness seemed to make the heartaches easier and the glad moments happier.

As Veterans Day weekend approached, I wondered if

Sharon would realize it was one year ago that she was injured.

The answer came when I found a piece of paper lying on her dresser, on which was written:

Les is nice. I love hem. Mother and
Father to. I want to go back to Lincoln.
Rich is nice. I talk to hem all the time.
I was hit my a car. To mory we be the
day I was hit.

9

Building Memories

ONE AFTERNOON I SUGGESTED TO SHARON that she go out and rake the leaves. "OK," she said. "Where's the rake?"

"It's probably in the garage, if you put it away when you used it Friday."

She returned in a few minutes with the broom in her hand. "I found it, Mother."

"That isn't the rake. That's the broom we sweep the kitchen with. Maybe you left the rake in the driveway. Go look."

A short time later she called in to me, "I found it, Mama." I glanced out the window and noted with satisfaction that she did have the rake. The booklet I had been reading, *Understanding Aphasia*, mentioned that one of the major deficiencies of the aphasic patient will be noticed in naming and identifying objects. I found so much in the booklet that helped me better understand

Sharon's problems. I knew I needed all the help I could get.

This need prompted my decision to respond to an announcement I noticed in the newspaper, of a day-long conference on "The Exceptional Child" at San Jose State College.

The morning session consisted of lectures and workshops. I chose a workshop led by the Speech Coordinator of the Palo Alto School District. After the session I talked to the leader who expressed genuine interest in Sharon's problems. One sentence she said still echoes in my mind; it no doubt planted the seed for this book. "You must keep a diary and record your experiences; don't you realize what your story could mean to others in similar circumstances?"

I left the conference that day with a thrilling thought. The gentle hand that constantly guided me had led me to that conference for a definite reason. Our struggle now had a new purpose, with the realization that we sought answers not just for our daughter, but for others in similar circumstances.

The recent visit to the neurosurgeon had impressed on me how few answers had been found even by the experts. "Why is it that Sharon seems to have a memory of her classmates and other friends, and her family, yet no memory of any events connected with them, or experiences in her past?" I asked him.

His reply startled me. "It just proves what I've said all along. No one really knows anything about the brain. The doctors who think they do are only kidding themselves."

As I thought about his statement now I felt awed by the realization that we were in a unique position to discover possible answers. Certainly I must remember to put in my diary experiences like our visit to friends the previous weekend.

We had known Guy and Wyoma for 27 years. When we first came to California as bride and groom we had lived in adjacent apartments, and a close friendship had developed and grown through the years. Their son, Henry, and our twins had been friends since early childhood. Guy and Wyoma had visited Sharon in the hospital, and had stopped by often since she had been home. They had never brought Henry with them, however, since they preferred that he not see her in such a condition. Sharon seemed to enjoy the visit. She conducted herself with more than usual poise, and talked quite sensibly to Henry. After we left she told me, "I don't remember ever having seen Henry before."

"Do you remember Guy and Wyoma?" I asked.

"Why of course, I've known them all my life."

Was there a clue to the answer for my question here? Did it hinge on the fact that memory of the parents had been kept alive by their visits? Was the memory of her school friends and family retained in the same way, by photos and visits, even when she seemed unaware of their presence?

I recorded the incident in my new diary, and also wrote some comments about our November 12 visit to the neurosurgeon. "Analyzing the doctor's attitude, I realize the change that has taken place. A few months ago his admission of any progress was always tempered with the statement, 'But you know, as I've told you before, her brain took a terrific beating, and there is just no way of knowing how far she can go. All we can do is hope and pray.' This time there was no such word of caution. Instead he told me: 'On your last two visits I have seen definite progress, and this time it is even more pronounced.' ''

A few days after our visit to Guy and Wyoma's a new crisis arose in Sharon's life. When we went to pick her up after her school classes we found her waiting at the door, so distraught that the school secretary was trying to console her. Little by little, between sobs, she managed to tell us what had happened. A short while earlier, angered because she had complained about the heavy cigarette smoke in the rest room, several girls grabbed and held her while some of the others blew smoke in her face and cursed her.

The next day she stayed home from school. Although she appeared extremely restless, not knowing what to do with her time, we did not feel we should try to persuade her to go back. We shared the fear she expressed in a trembling voice, that "they will try to take it out on me again, if I go back."

When the school principal called Charley and expressed his interpretation of the problem, "Sharon has too high ideals," we realized the futility of trying to discuss the problem with him. The school was in an old frame building that also housed an elementary school. There were strict regulations against smoking, and it seemed incredible to us that the principal could overlook the extreme fire hazard, the health factor, and interpret the problem to be "Sharon's high ideals." Perhaps he simply realized he couldn't control the students' smoking and chose to ignore it.

I felt we needed time to decide what further action to

take. In the meantime I'd try to keep Sharon occupied. "We'll leave home early tomorrow morning, and spend lots of time in the shopping center before going to Stanford. Would you like that, Sharon?"

"I sure would. Can I buy a purse to go with my red dress?"

"If we can find one that isn't too expensive."

We spent several enjoyable hours walking around the stores. Then we found a purse that suited Sharon and also my budget, and her happy voice attracted the attention of several passersby, "Oh, thank you so much, Mom. Won't Les be surprised when he sees my new purse? I can't wait to show it to him."

I looked at her excited face, and remembered the girl I had chased around the counters just a few months before. *What a wonderful improvement!* I thought. I noticed growth in so many areas.

The session at the Stanford clinic that afternoon reminded me that this growth was only a tiny beginning. A staggering amount of effort and a long, painful period of time would be required in the process of elementary education.

I again observed from the one-way window. The therapist showed Sharon the picture of a man making a phone call from a telephone booth, looking very distraught. His wrecked car stood outside.

"Tell me what the man in the picture is doing," said the therapist.

"He's telling jokes on the telephone."

She's trying to be funny, I thought. Then I realized she had given a serious answer, but completely missed the meaning of the picture.

91

The therapist then showed her one of a child drawing all over the wall, with an easel right by her. "She's drawing pictures," Sharon said.

The therapist told me later that one of their goals was to help her see the whole picture and interpret it correctly. I was deeply thankful for the expert help available through the Stanford speech clinic; but I knew Sharon must also have regular daily schooling. I prayed for guidance. Should I try to persuade her to go back to the continuation school? In spite of all our efforts, it seemed the only school available to us at present. I realized the risks involved, but did the educational opportunities outweigh the risks?

The answer came on her fourth day home. When we returned home from Stanford late in the afternoon, I noticed someone sitting on the porch. As we came closer I realized it was Angel, the one friend Sharon had made at school. I had met her a month or so earlier when she had visited Sharon and stayed for dinner with us. I could understand the friendship that had developed between the two, for I sensed the sincere concern and compassion for our hurt and lonely daughter that Angel felt. She had known little but hurts and loneliness in her lifetime. She was an orphan who had been shifted from one place to another. She had served time in juvenile halls, and still associated with rough gangs, yet she retained a soft, gentle quality.

Angel smiled at Sharon and told her: "I've been waiting a long time for you. I came over to persuade you to go back to school."

"I don't want to go back to that school; they will hurt me again."

"Look, you don't think I'd try to get you to go back if I thought you'd be hurt again, do you? I intend to see to it that those girls leave you alone." Her tone and manner gave assurance that she was quite capable of keeping her promise.

"Just try it for one day, and see if you don't want to continue. After that I promise I won't bug you again about it."

The eager way Sharon prepared for school the next morning convinced me she had wanted to be talked into going back. Protected by the guardian Angel God had supplied, she continued with her schooling. However, her longing to go to Lincoln became more and more apparent as the days passed. She often seemed depressed after visits from her friends. I knew she grieved because she couldn't go to school with them. I tried to plan activities we could enjoy together, to take her mind off it. One Friday we went to see a football game at Lincoln. The weather was unusually cold, and I shivered throughout the game. But Sharon enjoyed the excitement so much that I felt that my investment in time and discomfort was well worthwhile.

That evening she accompanied her father to the grocery store. Enroute she was telling him about the game, when suddenly she stopped short in the middle of a sentence and started pointing at something and exclaiming in excitement, "Look, Daddy, look! Those lights, all over that house. What is that for?"

"Those are Christmas lights, Honey; soon lots of other homes will be lighted up the same way, whole streets of them."

"Oh, Daddy, you're always kidding me! Tell me what that really was."

93

At home, Charley and I tried to explain what Christmas is, the reason for the lights, and the exchange of gifts. She listened wide-eyed, but we wondered how much she understood.

The whole weekend was a happy time for her. On Saturday we went shopping together. Christmas decorations hung everywhere, and I shared her excitement as she "oh'd and ah'd" and commented again and again, "How beautiful!"

She helped me select a storybook for Rickey and Sheri, and then said, "Now, Mother, I want to get you a Christmas present, and I don't want you to see it. So you let me shop by myself for a while."

After only a moment's hesitation, I agreed with Sharon's idea.

"All right. See that clock on the wall over there? It's 11:30 now. I'll be waiting here at the front of the store for you at 12 o'clock. In the meantime you shop anywhere in the store you want to."

I walked away from her, wondering if I should have left her alone, if I was taking too great a risk. Then I realized I hadn't made the decision by myself. Although I sometimes failed to recognize it, God's Spirit led me during those occasions when I had to make immediate decisions and there wasn't time to pray for specific guidance. Filled with the peace of this certain knowledge, I spent an enjoyable half hour in the book department, then walked to the front of the store.

I had just gotten there when I saw her coming, a package in her arms, and her face radiant.

"Hi, Mama. I sure hope you're going to like what I got you."

"I will, Dear." Of that I was certain.

I felt exhausted, but extremely happy, when we arrived home. The day had brought another first in the growth of our child.

10

"First" Christmas

ANTICIPATION AND PREPARATION FOR CHRISTMAS now
made each day bright and happy for Sharon. It spilled over
in excited chatter. "Do you think Rickey will like what I
got him?" "Won't Les be surprised?" "Don't come into
my room, Mama. I don't want you to see what I'm
wrapping."

Again and again I felt a tingling thrill when I heard her
remarks and watched her reactions. She had the fresh
excitement of a young child, yet showed emotions that
gave evidence of something deeper than childish feelings.

I wrote in our Christmas letter: "Our 16-year-old Sharon is preparing for Christmas with all the enthusiasm and
anticipation most of us once experienced but lost somewhere between babyhood and adulthood. You see, in a
way this will be her first Christmas. She has no memory of
any other Christmas, just as she has no memory of any
previous birthday, Halloween, or Thanksgiving. Each
one is a fresh, exciting experience."

She was invited to a party at Jeanne's house and returned with her arms loaded with gifts and joy reflected in her face. I doubt if any wrapped present could equal in value the gift of fellowship and acceptance given her that afternoon by six of her peers.

Never had I felt such gratitude for a complete family as I experienced that Christmas day. I awakened to the sound of Sharon's happy voice, "Merry Christmas, Mom."

We opened our presents that morning to the strains of "Silent Night, Holy Night," and my thoughts went back to Christmas a year ago. I remembered those unopened packages under the tree in Sharon's hospital room, and the soft-spoken words: "There will be other Christmases." This was one of those other chances. Few times in my life have compared with the indescribable joy of that moment.

11

Friends

IT ALWAYS SEEMS DIFFICULT to get back to routine after
the Christmas season, and that year it seemed even worse
than usual. My days were full to overflowing, and, in
addition, I was worried about Sharon.

I was concerned about the childish tantrums that were
becoming increasingly a part of Sharon's reaction to frustration or anger. I felt I must help her conquer them, but
how? Certainly the answer required wisdom greater than
mine, and again I looked to God for help.

Time and again I was reminded of the "nothingness"
of Sharon's knowledge of a year before, and the tremendous remaining gaps that would take years to fill in. Yet
she had learned so much and conducted herself so well in
some ways that I found it hard to realize the limitation of
her knowledge. I was often startled by her reactions.

One day she came running into the house and interrupted my conversation with Trudy, our neighbor.
"Mama, Mama, the baby is eating the mother up."

Trudy and I looked outside, and then burst into laughter. A mother was breast-feeding her baby in a car at the curb.

We tried to explain about nursing, but Sharon's comment was, "I think that's awful."

Her food combinations were always interesting. Potatoes might be covered with honey or jam; catsup was poured on almost anything, including chicken; mayonnaise was used on a variety of vegetables. Often she would forget that milk belongs on prepared cereal and would start eating it dry.

When she helped set the table, I had to watch that she didn't fill the salt shaker with sugar, or the sugar bowl with salt.

I could depend on her to bring in the clothes from the line and fold the towels neatly. She took good care of her clothes; yet I was likely to find my freshly ironed curtains crumpled from her sitting on them, the milk left out, the steam iron leaking, or a trail of mud on the rug.

She now asked endless questions, not only of the family, but of others as well, particularly Trudy and Elmer Carlson, our long-time neighbors, whom she called "my second family."

One day when she saw Trudy outside with their dog, Sharon asked, "What's the animal's name?"

"She's a dog, Sharon, and her name is Minnie."

"Did you have that dog before my accident?"

"Yes, we did."

"Had I seen her before my accident?"

"Yes, you had."

"I don't remember. What are you doing now?"

"I'm cutting off the dead flowers."

"Things die, don't they? Will the dog die?"

"Yes, she will, Sharon. She's getting old."

Similar dialogues on many and varied subjects took place between Sharon and her "second family," and nearly all of them contained the question, "Was that before or after my accident?" She seemed to be constantly trying to fill in the huge blanks in her memory. The Carlsons provided great support and understanding to her.

But we were acutely conscious that the very mention of "brain damage" frightened and repelled many other persons, even some close friends. No matter how unfair we felt it to be, we had to accept the fact that the term carried a stigma with it. We talked freely to Sharon about her brain damage as we would have talked about any type of physical injury. She had no cause to feel shame about it, and we felt our attitude would influence hers.

Often we chuckled together over her mistakes. One day we were waiting for a local bus in Palo Alto when a train passed. "That isn't our bus—but it's a boat," she said. Then her gay laugh rang out, "That's the wrong word, isn't it? It's a car . . . tr . . . train." She looked at me with a pleased expression that she had gotten the right word. Many times her sense of humor and the ability to laugh at herself proved to be the needed antidote for frustration and despair.

One subject I tried not to let myself dwell on kept surfacing at times, and I wrote in my diary: "As long as I don't let myself compare Sharon today with what she was prior to the accident, I don't give way to discouragement. If I only compare with a year ago, or a few months ago, I can take pride in her progress, but when I let myself think of what a difference there would be had the accident not occurred, then the lump in my throat nearly chokes me.''

Many times I had to pray that God would help me keep the right attitude, and often the answers came in subtle, quiet ways. Like the time when the mother of one of Sharon's schoolmates at Lincoln called and told me she wanted to take us to Stanford for Sharon's next speech therapy visit. ''It will give us a chance to visit and will be a change from the long bus ride.'' My spirits always lifted after such times, and I thanked God for thoughtful friends.

12

Growing Pains

I DECIDED IT WAS TIME to take my crusade for Sharon's schooling to Lincoln High School again. This time I was more fortunate as I was able to talk directly to the principal and the girls' counselor, Miss Thompson. They both felt that all the noncurriculum classes (arts, crafts, gym, etc.) were so large that the teachers would not be able to give Sharon the attention she would require.

We then hit on the idea of a typing class, and they agreed to investigate to see if it would be possible for Sharon to enroll in it.

When the call finally came, telling me Sharon could join the typing class, I could hardly wait to tell her. I kept glancing at the clock; the hour before she was due home passed so slowly.

Sharon was ecstatic when I told her she could start her class the next week. Sobs and laughter shook her body, and I realized again how much this meant to her. When she regained her composure her excited voice rang through the room.

"I hope Les comes right home from school today. I can't wait to tell him—and Rich and Jeanne and Lynda and Joanne."

I thanked God for this answer to prayer, then added another request—that Sharon would be prepared to accept any disappointment that might await her.

Would Sharon be accepted now? I wondered. She referred to Lincoln as "my school, all my friends go there." Yet in the year and a half since her accident, she had lost contact with most of her former classmates. Returning to Lincoln would demand some adjustments. How could I prepare her for them?

Something occurred the next day that prepared Sharon in a better way than anything I could have said. She blurted out the details the moment she came in from school.

"Daddy stopped by the bakery on the way home today to get doughnuts, and there was a bunch of girls from Lincoln in there. Lynda and Gerry were with them. I was so glad to see Lynda, but she hardly spoke to me; didn't talk to me at all." Her lips quivered; I could tell she was having difficulty keeping back tears. "But Gerry talked to me. She acted real friendly."

Here, I thought, is the answer to my question. Some students, perhaps even some of those who have been her closest friends, will be embarrassed by her childish behavior and ignore her. But there will be others who will find satisfaction in helping one of their peers by friendly acceptance. They will compensate for the others.

As summer approached, excitement and busy preparation filled our days. We planned a trip, by train, to visit relatives and friends in Texas, Iowa, Wisconsin, Indiana, and Kentucky. Sharon asked many questions: "Is it the same date where we are going as it is here?" "Will they remember me even though I don't remember them?" "Did they have Easter there at the same time we did?" "Can I walk around on the train?"

I felt grateful that the trip occupied so much of our thinking, for I had become increasingly disturbed by a problem that I didn't know how to deal with.

Sharon resented the frequent visits of our three grandchildren, and showed her displeasure in varied ways. Sometimes if she found them here when she returned from school, she stalked off again after shouting: "I never can study here. They make too much noise and bother me too much." Then she would walk to our branch library, ten blocks away, to "study." She accomplished very little homework there, however. Other times she would just pick at them constantly, or bawl Stella out. "Your brats always mess up the house. Why do you have to come over here all the time?"

I tried to reason with Sharon about it, pointing out that they were just normal, active children who needed a lot of attention and love. I suggested she help me by talking to them or playing with them. She did seem to try to "be nice," but at times she gave vent to her feelings.

One Sunday Sharon's friends, Lynda and Joanne, dropped by while I was preparing dinner. Stella, Les, and Sharon were in the kitchen visiting with them when Rickey barged in. Holding Les' bat and glove, he interrupted the conversation, wanting Les to come out and play ball.

With no warning, Sharon reached over and dug her nails into his arm, drawing blood.

"Why in the world did you do that?" I angrily asked.

"I can't even have my friends over without them bothering us," she yelled. "They get on my nerves."

I lost my temper and slapped her, hard. That triggered a violent reaction from Sharon. She hit me several times and tried to scratch. Stunned, I ordered her to her room. Her father came in and steered her to it.

Les took Rickey outside to play ball, and the rest were shocked into silence. Finally I asked, "Lynda, would you go in and talk to Sharon, then bring her back out here with you?"

Some ten minutes later they emerged, and one look at Sharon told me the storm was over.

"Lynda, what would your mother do if you ever hit her?" I asked.

Lynda's quick reply left no doubt of her feelings on the matter. "Oh, I can't imagine even thinking of hitting my mother."

Joanne added, "Oh, I might think about it, and sometimes I might want to, but I'd never dare."

The incident left a mark on all of us.

I lay awake that night pondering all the facets of the problem. Sharon had displayed traits that I knew had to be dealt with firmly. From my reading and observation of other brain-damaged persons, I knew the dangers— jealousy, resentment, selfishness, and violence. But what could I do about them? As I groped for an answer, a long-cherished Bible verse came to mind, "If any of you lack wisdom, let him ask of God, that giveth to all men liberally, and upbraideth not; and it shall be given him."

I repeated it silently several times, letting the meaning of the words sink into my consciousness. "O Lord," I prayed, "I'm heartsick, ashamed and confused. You know all about it, and You know how completely I lost my temper. Forgive me, Lord. Give me a giant portion of patience, understanding, and wisdom. I need them so desperately. Please still this raging tumult within me and bring quietness so I may hear You."

Since that afternoon I have never used any physical punishment on Sharon, nor has she displayed any tendency to violence.

Our vacation trip that summer brought relief to tense nerves, and relaxation for tired bodies. Most important, it gave Sharon the sense of belonging to a large family of relatives who loved and accepted her without reservation. I doubt if anything else could have meant so much to her at that time.

We came home refreshed in mind and body. Sharon had collected many wholesome memories to help fill the voids, and I realized more than ever how valuable these jewels of memory are to all of us.

One of the greatest benefits I received was in the form of a rebuke from Helen, my brother's wife. I had told her how concerned I was about schooling for Sharon, that we couldn't send her back to the continuation school again, since even the principal there said he felt she shouldn't return. "The doctors at Stanford considered the placement to be completely wrong, too," I said. "But there doesn't seem to be any place else for her. I don't know what we are going to do."

Helen turned from the stove and looked me in the eye. "Now, Lucille, you know God wouldn't bring Sharon this far, in such a marvelous fashion, then fail to provide schooling for her.''

I have often recalled her words. At times when I have let doubt enter my mind, they have reminded me that God has never failed to provide.

13

School Days

As the time approached for school to open, I looked eagerly for God's answer. I expected to hear from our district administration office, but no word came. For some reason, I didn't feel I should contact them. Instead I had the distinct impression that I should send Sharon to Lincoln the opening day.

She liked the idea and waved to me with a happy grin when she climbed into the car. I felt anything but happy, realizing the commotion our action might trigger at Lincoln, and the effect it might have on Sharon. Yet I had asked for God's guidance, and felt that I was following it.

Miss Thompson didn't take long to get in touch with me that morning. The phone rang within an hour after Sharon left home. "You know we can't register Sharon here," the agitated Miss Thompson told me. "If we allow her to attend any classes, there will have to be special arrangements made with the teachers, and we will have to confer with the district administration about it."

My answer was emphatic. "How long will that take? This is her school district, you know, and she isn't registered at any other school. I believe we are within our constitutional rights to expect you to provide educational opportunities for Sharon." My hands shook so I could hardly hold the phone, but I managed to keep my voice steady.

"You've put me in a very bad spot by sending her; will you please come for her?" She paused for my reply.

"She knows the way. You can tell her to walk home. But we'll be expecting to hear from you in the next day or two."

Soon after Sharon arrived, Charley and I took her to the district administration office. The three of us sat down with the man in charge of special cases. We had talked to him on previous occasions about our dissatisfaction with her placement. "We've come to find out what you have planned for Sharon this year," I said.

He looked startled, then admitted, "You've caught me cold; I haven't considered the matter. How old are you, Sharon?"

I had the feeling that he hoped she would say 18, then he would be off the hook. When she told him she was 17 he said, "I believe you attended the continuation school last year, and also one class at Lincoln. How did you get along?"

She answered without hesitation, "Lincoln was fine; but not that pa-ro-lee school."

He then asked Sharon to go out and sit in the waiting room while we talked. "We have waited a full year for adequate help from our district," Charley said. "We don't feel that the continuation school was the proper

110

place for her and we don't intend to be put off much longer."

"From an educational standpoint it was proper placement."

"Would you want your daughter there under the same circumstances?" I asked.

After a long pause, he shook his head. "I can't answer that." I felt we had made our point.

He then telephoned the principal at Lincoln, who promised to make arrangements for a conference with us the next afternoon.

I didn't sleep much that night; the day's events had left me mentally and physically drained, and I dreaded the conference. Yet I had the gentle assurance of God's leading. He seemed especially close during that long night.

Sharon started back to Lincoln the next week on a month's trial basis. They had wanted to schedule only nonacademic classes, but upon our insistence they included three academic subjects: remedial, noncredit classes in English and social studies, and a regular life science.

My diary reads:

Sharon has been in Lincoln four and one-half weeks, and I see definite progress. How I hope she can continue there. The first week was rather difficult. She arrived home the first day without her English and social studies books. She had left them in Miss Thompson's office, and it was several days before they were returned to her. Her crafts and sewing classes were changed to different rooms after she had been there a few days, and this confused her. Several times she had difficulty finding them. But now she is having no problem at all in that respect. She lost her purse one day (had left it in her last classroom when she went to a rally). She appeared quite worried about it when she arrived home, but didn't want me to go to school with her the next day to help her locate it. She found it without assistance.

Sharon and I now spent many hours each day on her homework. I read the assigned pages to her; and often I would write down the answers to questions and she would copy them. We went over and over spelling words. Many nights I had to insist that she put away her books and go to bed.

Prior to our second conference, late in October, we requested written reports from the teachers for Miss Thompson to share at our meeting. The ones from her crafts teacher and her sewing teacher were read first and I almost gave way to despair. They both expressed the definite conclusion that she did not belong in a regular classroom, that she took entirely too much of their time, and that of the other students in trying to help her.

The reports from the English and social studies teacher were more positive. "Although Sharon isn't able to keep up with the normal work, she is so eager and tries so hard that I feel she should be allowed to stay."

After a long silence I inquired, "Where is the report from Mr. Brink, her life science teacher?"

Miss Thompson looked startled. "You know we were unable to get her in that class. We couldn't arrange her schedule to work it in."

"She's been in life science all the time," I told the astonished counselor.

"Oh, I didn't know that. I'll go see if I can get a report from him."

A strange excitement stirred within me as we waited, and the familiar phrase popped into my mind: "God works in mysterious ways His wonders to perform."

When Miss Thompson returned she told us, "He's coming in to give his report in person."

When he arrived, I spoke up, "Mr. Brink, the purpose of this conference is to determine if Sharon takes too much of the teacher's time in a normal classroom."

"That isn't the question I'm concerned about," he said. "What I wonder is whether or not it is too frustrating for her to be unable to keep up with the class."

"She has been happier since she started back to Lincoln than she has at any time since the accident. She says your class seems only about fifteen minutes long."

"That confirms my opinion that the class is good for her, if for no other reason than the give and take with her peers. What's more, I'm convinced that her being there is good for the other students. They need the experience of helping someone else."

After further discussion, it was agreed that the crafts and sewing would be dropped at the end of the quarter, but that she would continue English, social studies, and life science. In addition, we would hire a tutor, if we could find one, to work with Sharon an hour a day at the school.

I left the conference that day with a sense of awe, realizing how God had been at work in Sharon's behalf. I felt deeply grateful to the human instruments He had used. I wondered who had maneuvered the schedule to include life science; I still don't know, but that person is high on my list of those I look forward to thanking someday.

With help from the school district we found a tutor, a young woman with a pleasant manner who we felt would work well with our daughter and also with the school administration.

Sharon's classes now began at 9 a.m. and finished at 1:15. Homework consumed many afternoon and evening hours for both of us. Of course I realized she was actually learning very little about social studies or life science, but I felt the practice in writing and spelling and the brain activity it stimulated made the effort worthwhile. Some of the books I had read cited the theory that, with much repetition, other brain cells could be trained to take over the work of permanently damaged ones. I fervently hoped that this would happen in Sharon's case.

14

Answers

SHORTLY AFTER SHARON'S "SECOND CHRISTMAS" I
noticed an announcement in the paper that Dr. Rafferty,
the state superintendent of schools, was scheduled to
speak to the parents' group in a nearby school, and the
public was invited. I felt I should go, although I didn't
quite know why. After the speech, Dr. Rafferty invited
questions from the audience and I jumped at the chance.
"I am the mother of a 17-year-old girl who suffered severe
brain damage when struck by a car two years ago," I said.
"We are experiencing great difficulty in finding educational help for her. Is the state making any studies on brain
damage, and is any consideration being given to providing
help for this group?"

"Yes, we are making some studies in this regard, and
help is in the planning stage," he answered. "If you will
write me a letter, marking it 'personal,' I'll see that it gets
to the person in charge of this area."

I wrote the letter the next day, giving details about

Sharon's ability before the accident, the severity of the injury, her progress, our search for education, and cited all the problems, including the need for physical education. I mentioned that we were grateful that she was now being allowed to take classes at Lincoln. Then I expressed our primary concern. "Sharon will be 18 this July, and her reeducation is just gaining momentum. Of course the question in our minds is, where do we go from here? Private tutors, in addition to being terribly expensive, are difficult to secure. The one we have now is pregnant and will be able to continue only a few more months. Does the California Department of Education have an answer for us, and for many other parents with similar problems? We feel your answer will, in so many cases, be the difference between such accident victims being a contribution to, or a drag on, society."

The result of that letter was an astonishing phone call two weeks later. "Mrs. Gardner, I'm Dr. Outland, a consultant in the California Department of Education. I am calling from Lincoln High School, where I have just finished a fine conference with the administration of the school and the district regarding your daughter. I would like to come by your home and talk to you if it is convenient."

I assured him that it was convenient, and when I greeted him at the door I immediately sensed his sincerity and empathy. I became more and more encouraged as he talked. "The teachers seem to think Sharon is getting so much out of the classes. The school will be glad to have her come back for three more years if she wants to. I saw her folder, and am especially pleased and surprised at her handwriting."

We discussed physical education for Sharon; I mentioned that her doctors felt this to be most necessary, but that the school had so far refused to let her in a physical education class.

"This is a new experience for the school," he said. "I feel they are to be commended for trying it, and for their interest in Sharon."

Before he left he gave me his business card, telling me to be sure to write him if I had any questions, or if a problem came up.

I watched his car pull away from the curb with many thoughts dancing in my brain. That's why God "nudged" me to attend that parents' meeting. Of course, he's right that Lincoln should be commended, considering society's attitude toward brain damage. I wonder if Sharon will want to go back there after all her friends have graduated. With interest from the state level we may find a different attitude on the part of our district. Maybe this will pave the way for others who need similar help; there must be many of them considering the large numbers of persons injured in accidents every day. Excitement and challenge surged within me.

When I told Sharon about his visit and mentioned that he had said she could go back to Lincoln for three more years, a frown clouded her face. "I hope I don't have to go more than one more year. All my friends will be gone and I won't know anybody. Besides, I'll be a lot older than everybody."

Jeanne came over that evening, and I heard her assuring Sharon, "Why, you know a lot of juniors and sophomores," and she named some of them. Her faithful friendship smoothed many rough places for Sharon.

117

15

"Not One of the Graduates, But..."

THE CLASS OF 1964 was Sharon's class, and as graduation approached, she experienced many difficult times. While her twin and all her friends prepared for the big event, she continued the struggle to learn to read and write. I knew she cried inwardly at being left out, and her brave efforts to cover up for my sake touched me deeply. Often when I kissed her good night I found her pillow wet with tears.

She was also experiencing the hurt of being left out at church. I tried to analyze why the attitude among her peer group there had changed. Many times since the accident I had been grateful for the consideration given her, and the thoughtful manner in which she had been included in the varied activities. I knew it put added responsibilities on the sponsors, and I had often expressed my appreciation to them. But now some of the group seemed to make deliberate attempts to hurt her—and they succeeded, again and again.

She didn't very often tell me about it, but one Sunday evening when she came to sit by me in church with her eyes red from crying, she blurted out, "When I started to sit down by one of the girls in the meeting she told me not to sit there, and then I started to sit in another seat, and another girl told me the same thing. Why don't they like me? I try to be nice."

Our daughter's tutor listened to Sharon's problems sympathetically. Sometimes Sharon wept in her class. Her tutor's quiet understanding made it possible for Sharon to unload, and I felt grateful. I knew it was much better that she let her feelings out than to keep them bottled up inside.

Sharon missed the attention she had formerly received from her twin. A part-time job in a meat market, preparing for graduation, and writing letters kept Les rushing. The recipient of his letters, Paula Voyles, would be a 1964 graduate from Atwater High School, which was some 75 miles away.

Although Sharon couldn't participate in the excitement of graduation, she entered wholeheartedly into other preparations being made at our home. I felt thankful that all the activity kept Sharon from dwelling on the hurt she experienced when she had to be a spectator rather than a participant.

Lincoln holds its graduation exercises outdoors in the Municipal Rose Garden, just two blocks from the school. Sharon kept urging us, "Hurry up, or we won't get any seats," and pleaded to her father, "Please, Daddy, don't be late like you always are." The ceremonies started at 6:30, and she sighed in relief when we settled into our places a little after 6. She didn't stay seated long, however. In a few minutes, she stood up. "Save my seat for me, I'm going to see some of my friends. I'll be back soon."

"Where are you going? I think you'd better stay here," Charley said. But she kept going and soon vanished in the crowd. "We shouldn't have let her go. She'll be a nuisance," he said. I knew it, yet I couldn't deny her the small pleasure of mingling with the graduates for a little while.

I became increasingly nervous, however, as the minutes passed and she hadn't returned. I heard the first strains of the processional, and turned around for an anxious look. Then I saw Sharon, marching back to where we were seated, barely a pace ahead of the marching graduates.

I could tell tears were close to the surface when she took her seat beside us. She sat quietly through the ceremonies, but from her expression I knew the heartache she experienced. It was no easy matter for Sharon to sit in the audience while her classmates were receiving their diplomas.

Some ten days before the opening of the fall term, Charley and I, accompanied by Sharon, went to the school for a conference with three Lincoln staff members and a representative of the district.

The most important thing on my mind was the matter of a physical education class for Sharon. "From many sources I have learned that physical exercise is most important in stimulating brain activity," I explained. "We feel that a lack of proper exercise is the main cause for Sharon having gained too much weight. Both her neurosurgeon and internist feel that P.E. is of utmost

121

importance. Dr. Outland told us that the state provides funds for special P.E. classes for the handicapped, but our district has failed to take advantage of this. Since there are no special classes, we feel Sharon should be allowed in the regular classes.''

''Have you considered fully the possibility of her being injured in gym?'' the district representative asked with concern in his voice.

''Yes, I have—just like I fully realized the risk the first time we left her at home alone, the first time she went to town, or the first ball game she attended by herself. Yet I felt they were all necessary steps in Sharon's growth. In each instance I have sought God's guidance in choosing the right time. I'm convinced, despite the risks, that Sharon should have P.E. this semester.''

Miss Thompson spoke up. ''I am too. I opposed her taking it last year, but I feel differently about it now. I certainly don't want to have to tell Sharon no; she has her heart so set on it.''

I recalled what another member of the Lincoln staff had told me in June: ''In a discussion I had with Miss Thompson about Sharon, we both agreed that it has been good for the school to have had Sharon here this year.''

The district representative finally agreed, providing we signed papers stating that neither the teacher nor the school would be responsible in case of an accident. We were willing to fulfill that request, so the problem was resolved.

With that settled, we worked out the rest of Sharon's schedule. She would attend school from 9 a.m. to 2:15 each day, taking basic math, P.E., English, social studies, and life science.

My sister-in-law's words again came to mind as we left the school. God was still providing for Sharon's education, and I breathed a prayer of thanks.

16

The Valley Handys

TOWARD THE END OF OCTOBER, Sharon came storming in from school one afternoon, an hour late. "I went into the office to ask them if I would graduate this year. They told me I don't have enough credits. I don't see why. Most kids only go four years to high school. I don't see why I have to go so much longer."

"Now, Sharon, I thought you understood that when I explained it to you the other day. You were out of school nearly a whole year when you were hurt. Then you had to relearn everything, and that takes time. You are doing so well . . . . "

The door to her room slammed shut. What can I do or say? I wondered. She simply won't accept the fact that her education has barely begun.

She did study hard, though, and week after week I noted steady improvement. One day she held a new book out to me when she arrived from school. "Mr. Stevenson told me I can raise my grade to a B in English if I do homework each night from this book. I sure want to.''

Her sparkling eyes left no doubt about how much the grade meant to her. I realized more than ever her anguish over the many D's and E's she had received since returning to Lincoln.

I also became increasingly aware of another source of unhappiness. She had become the object of taunts by some of the male students. She did not often tell me about it, but many times I sensed the reason for her thinly veiled hurts.

She did talk, loud and long, about the most crushing blow to her morale. She came into the kitchen one evening in tears.

"Why didn't Les tell me he and Paula are engaged? I'm his twin and everybody else knew about it before I did."

"Honey, that isn't true. Only a very few people know about it. I found out just a few days ago. You weren't here when they told me. They intended . . .''

"Well, Lynda knew and she mentioned it to me on the phone; she thought I knew about it.''

I made another attempt to soothe her, "Please don't take it so hard. They were going to tell you as soon as they had an opportunity. Neither Paula nor Les would intentionally slight you." But she refused to be comforted by my words.

"I was the one that introduced them, when Paula visited our Sunday school class at Christmas vacation. Now I wish I hadn't. Les never talks to me anymore.''

"Well, he doesn't talk to me much either, except to say, 'I'm hungry. What's to eat?' He's really awfully busy, with his classes at City College and his job . . . ''

"Well, he has plenty of time for Paula.''

126

"They don't plan to be married for at least two years. He'll be around for a long time yet," I said.

"Well, I don't care whether he's here or not."

But I knew she did care. She depended on Les in so many ways. She discussed problems, real or imaginary, with him, always ending with the question, "What would you do, Les?" She poured out her hurts to him, and his dry wit soon had her laughing, no matter what her original mood.

I knew Les lectured her sternly about her growing tendency to try to attract attention from the boys, often in a clumsy, childish way. I was worried about this boy-crazy phase and appreciated his efforts, since I knew his words would have more effect on her than ours would.

Sharon soon got over her hurt with Les. It is to her credit that she always bounced back, and refused to give in to depression for long.

I felt thankful for this trait time and again as the days passed. Without it I doubt if she could have maintained her normally happy disposition. The taunts at school continued and the deliberate slights at church increased. I could understand that the College and Careers Group would feel she didn't belong with them, but I couldn't understand how some of its members could invite Les to a social function and completely ignore his twin standing by him.

Then, at a time when she most needed it, she found acceptance in a group that provided even more than recreation and companionship. The Valley Handys is an organization of physically handicapped persons whose motto is "We Help Each Other." Through it we became acquainted with a world of which we had been totally ignorant. There, among people who talked and joked and thoroughly enjoyed life despite their crippling, and often painful, disabilities, Sharon learned lessons of far more value than any she had learned in school. How could she feel sorry for herself when she observed them? "I'm so lucky," she would say. "I can walk and jump and run and take care of myself, and go where I want to. I have so many friends who have to stay in a wheelchair. Some of them can't even feed themselves. I sure have a lot to be thankful for."

17

Pomp and Circumstance

WHEN IT CAME TIME to think about school for the fall again, Sharon was adamant. "I don't want to go back to Lincoln. I'm older than the rest of the kids and some of them make fun of me."

After checking with the County Superintendent of Schools, I learned that a full program of Adult Education classes was offered. I made an appointment for mid-August, when the fall schedules would be out and then requested Lincoln to send a transcript of Sharon's credits. This would include her freshman year, when she had earned better-than-average grades, the ones from the continuation school, and the few from the last two years at Lincoln.

Sharon seemed nervous when we waited in the reception room that morning. She talked in a loud tone, reverting to her old habit of attracting attention. "If I go to Adult Education, can I get a high school diploma? I don't want to go if I can't."

Our interview with Dr. McCall, the principal, went well. There would be no problem with Sharon starting classes.

I left his office with a full schedule of classes for Sharon in my purse.

During the bus ride home, Sharon kept talking about all the news she had to tell Les and her daddy. "Won't they be surprised that I am going to take art? That's going to be fun. I just can't wait to tell them about my diploma."

"Now, Honey, remember what Dr. McCall said about your having to pass some tests, and also get passing grades in all your classes in order to earn the diploma." I didn't want to dim her enthusiasm, but I didn't want her to count too much on it, either. "It's going to be difficult, you know. I don't want you to be too disappointed if you don't make it."

"You said you'd find a tutor to help me, and I don't mind working real hard for it."

She did work hard, and so did Don Kruse, the energetic young teacher we hired to help her. I spent many hours assisting with the studies he planned for her. Tests proved to be her biggest problem. So often she failed to understand what was required, and became extremely nervous and upset. But she stuck with it, and managed to acquire credits with D or C- grades.

Sharon was always ready to join in any extra activity, so when the young people at our church were asked to write letters, each no longer than one page in length, telling why they thought their mother should be honored on Mother's Day, she set to work on hers right away. The finished essay was entirely her own doing, mispelled words and all.

130

The mothers were presented with their daughters' letters on that special Sunday. Mine remains one of my most treasured possessions. She used every inch of space on the typewriter-size page. Her second sentence, which stands out above all the rest for me, reads: "I love her." She also wrote: "My mother lived at the hospital. She slept on a couch only four or five hours a night. After I came home from the hospital she watched after me all the time. I had to go to Standford all year for speech tharpy. I had to take the gray hound bus so my mom went with me so I won't have to get scared our lost . . . . Since I got out of school early I a lote of times got restless so my mom went shopping with me even when she had a lot of washing to do and housecleaning. Then when she was trying to do these thinks she would baby sit for my sister when she was going to go to work . . . . At night our street is real dark. If I every had to be home by myself I get scared to death. In my mind I think there is a lot of kooks our spokes. So if my dad and brother are gone and my mom has a school class to go to our some place else she just stays home instead . . . . A lot of moms wouldn't watche me as good as she does."

As graduation approached, an air of excitement prevailed. Presents arrived from near and far. Sharon received her cap and gown several days early, and we took pictures. During the morning worship service, on the Sunday before commencement, our pastor presented each graduate with a book. I am sure no parent watched with more pride than I did as they lined up, facing the congregation, at the front of the sanctuary. Sharon stood toward the end. I studied her face as she waited for her turn, and thought with a sickening feeling—she's getting nervous. Then, to my horror, she started giggling. That moment when she had most wanted to act mature, childhood had claimed her again.

"What makes me laugh like that when I'm trying to be serious?" she asked me later.

"It's because you feel embarrassed. It happens to everyone occasionally. Don't let it worry you too much."

On Tuesday the temperature soared to 99 degrees during the afternoon, and our Civic Auditorium felt uncomfortably warm that graduation evening. However, the heat didn't dim the enthusiasm of the more than 1,500 people who shared with us the thrill of watching a loved one receive a diploma.

At the first strains of "Pomp and Circumstance" I swallowed hard. Then as the 440 black-robed graduates filed by, I caught a glimpse of the expressions on the faces of men and women of all ages and of many nationalities, and sensed their joy and pride of accomplishment.

The letdown that usually follows high-school graduation was tempered for Sharon by anticipation of a 12-day vacation she had scheduled for late June at Easter Seal Camp. This would be the first time since her accident that she had been away from us longer than overnight. Only a few times had she spent a night with girl friends or relatives. I knew she felt excited, yet a little apprehensive, about being away so long. Some of her friends from Valley Handys would be there, though, and she'd make new friends.

I had different feelings, however, about the scheduled departure of her twin. Les had joined the Marine Corps Reserve, and would leave in mid-July for six months of active duty. I knew he faced a difficult three months of basic training, and also the ever-present possibility of being sent to Vietnam if the situation there grew worse.

As my mind focused again and again on my desperate desire for his safety, I realized anew the necessity for my utter dependence on God's protection. Then I wondered, how could any mother endure a similar situation without faith in God? My gratitude for faith and hope found expression in prayer: "Thank You, Lord, for assurance of Your watch care over both of our precious twins as they face these new experiences."

18

Her Own Place

SHARON TELEPHONED US FREQUENTLY from camp, sometimes twice a day. She'd never admit to being homesick,
but always had something "important" to tell us.

On one occasion she told me, in an indignant tone,
"We're supposed to take a nap every afternoon. I don't
like to take naps. I'm not a baby. Sometimes I slip out of
my room when we're supposed to be sleeping. Today a
counselor saw me and sent me back. They watch you too
much here."

Thank goodness for that, I thought.

When she returned home, letter writing occupied much
of her time. She had promised to write several of her new
friends and she wrote long letters to Les several times a
week. For more than two years she had been correspond-
ing with Jerry, a former neighbor, now in the service. His
long, newsy letters told her of the faraway places he
visited. He encouraged her in her studies, asked questions

so she would have something to write back, and sent snapshots. In short, Jerry showed his concern for her in the most practical ways he could think of.

Sharon participated in the handicapped swim sessions at the YMCA twice a week, went bowling with them, and attended their once-a-month socials. At one of the socials she met 18-year-old Don, who had been confined to a wheelchair with paralysis on the right side since being struck while riding on his motorcycle several years before.

She wheeled him around all afternoon. Two days later his mother called and told me: "Sharon has given Don the motivation he's needed for a long time. Yesterday he got out of his wheelchair and managed to walk around holding onto the furniture. He also worked harder than usual at his studies."

When I repeated the conversation to Sharon she smiled and said, "It sure makes me feel good to be able to help handicapped people."

I became increasingly aware that a feeling of acceptance brought out the best performance and behavior in Sharon, while she responded to a sense of rejection by becoming pushy and showing off childishly. I particularly noticed this reaction at church. I knew it hampered her progress, but didn't know what to do about it.

Then one of her friends from the handicapped group accompanied her to the Sunday school class and some of the young people's activities. His disability made speech difficult, but in a few words he voiced what I had felt for a long time. "Sharon won't continue to improve unless she attends a different church group."

I knew he was right.

He then told me, in short phrases, with long pauses, about the singles group in a large downtown church that he had recently joined.

Sharon flashed me a persuasive smile, and her eyes danced as she asked, ''May I go there next Sunday, Mom?''

''I don't know yet, but I'll think about it.''

I did think about it; in fact the pros and cons of the matter occupied my mind all that week. Each new step for Sharon held an element of danger; would this be taking too great a risk? There would be a particular problem of transportation.

I also suspected that our daughter might have plenty to say if she received a no answer. I sensed a growing rebellion in her, and a determination to start making some of her own decisions. So far I'd been able to get her to accept the ones she didn't like by explaining to her the reasons behind them. She knew I loved her dearly, and wanted only the best for her, and she loved me. This alone kept the rebellion in check. In a few months her chronological age would be 21. Yet she had only five years of memory and experience on which to base her decisions.

Sunday came and I still didn't know what to do, but I soon found that Sharon had made plans of her own. ''Vic is coming by to take me to Sunday school, and I'll take the bus home after church,'' she informed me. Vic, another member of the Valley Handys, also belonged to the singles group.

She came home bubbling with enthusiasm. ''They have a great big class and everyone is so friendly. I want to go there all the time.''

Sharon continued going to the group, and when I saw indications of the return of self-confidence, as the weeks and months passed, I felt glad that we hadn't prevented her from making the change.

After a year with the singles group, she became acquainted with some of the members of the College and Careers group in the church. They gave her a cordial invitation to transfer to their group, since most of the singles were older than Sharon. She made the transfer, and entered into their activities with a spirit of enthusiasm and zeal.

Sharon didn't want to return to a full schedule of classes that fall, and I didn't insist. She enrolled in a three-hour art course two afternoons a week. She usually went by bus, and had to transfer. I admired her determination, since she had to transport all her supplies back and forth each day that she went.

During the summer she had started doing volunteer work in a small local hospital, and now in addition to that she started working part time two days a week at the American Cancer Society. She worked conscientiously at her volunteer job of stamping the literature with the address of the local branch.

An important event took place that fall—Les and Paula's wedding. Paula had asked Sharon to be in charge of the guest book and she wanted to look her best. She chose an orange chiffon dress with flattering lines. The color highlighted the sparkle in her eyes and the color in her face. She performed her job well, and kept her composure throughout the ceremony.

I felt grateful that Sharon's full schedule helped to take her mind off her missing twin. I realized, though, with deep thankfulness, that she didn't need his shoulder to weep on as often now. The hope I had nourished for so long was rapidly becoming reality—she was beginning to find her own place in life.

19

"What Would I Have Been?"

I SPENT MANY HOURS trying to answer one question Sharon asked me in the spring of 1972. One evening she talked by phone to Joanne's mother and learned that the current issue of *Vogue* contained a picture of Joanne, who now lived in Texas and worked as a model. Sharon had recently learned that Lynda was engaged to a young man who would soon be graduated from medical school. She knew of the successes of many of her former classmates.

At breakfast the next morning I could tell she felt depressed about something. "What do you think I might have been if the accident hadn't happened?" she finally asked.

I groped for an adequate answer, then shook my head. "I don't know, Darling."

When she left for school, the question kept bothering me. Thoughts flashed through my mind as I pondered it. I found pencil and paper and started trying to put my thoughts into words. Over the next few weeks I jotted down thoughts as they came to me, and finally I completed "A Letter to Our Daughter."

Dearest Sharon:

The question you blurted out this morning is still echoing in my mind. I wanted to answer you in a way that would be reassuring, but I couldn't find the right words then, and I'm not sure I can now, but I must try.

That agonized question: "What might I have done with my life if the accident hadn't happened?" must haunt you often. I see it in your eyes when you learn of the achievements of your former classmates, and when you are shunned and rejected by those from whom you so desire acceptance and respect. I know you feel defeated when you are unable to carry on a conversation or perform a task on a par with your peers. I am aware of your attempts to cover up your feelings for my sake, just as you have an uncanny way of seeing through me when I try to hide my fatigue or irritations.

I realize your frustration and discouragement over having to strive hard to learn seventh-grade schoolwork long after your girlhood friends have completed college. Yet those of us who have watched your courageous struggle realize that you have made a much greater achievement by learning to read even one sentence than your former classmates have made in earning their college diplomas.

You have overcome tremendous obstacles, and made amazing progress. The only explanation I can give for your reaching the point where you are today is that God has kept His hand on you, and on me, in a very special way.

142

From that first night when you lay so close to death and God gave me the definite assurance that you were going to be all right, I have never ceased to marvel and be awed by the very real and constant presence of the Holy Spirit, gently guiding and directing. His presence filled the hospital room those ten long weeks you struggled for life, and He remained very close when we brought you home.

Certainly with only my own strength and intelligence I could not have nursed the pathetic creature you were then, and I knew of no human to whom I could turn for instructions in your care. The sense of awe I feel even now as I think about it makes every fiber in my being tingle. I experience the same thrill each time I think of how you've been protected all these ten years.

There are so many hazards in our world today for any young person, Sharon, and they are greatly multiplied for you. Whether you're aware of it or not, Honey, you've had a Guardian all those times you thought you were on your own. I can still remember the first time we left you at home by yourself. Your dad and I went grocery shopping for a short while one afternoon about two years after your accident. When we returned you said: "Thank you, Mother, for leaving me by myself." Well, I hadn't really left you alone then, nor have I in all the many times since then when you've been out of my sight. I continually petition God to let His Spirit be your constant Companion and Guide, and I am certain He's with you every second.

Since I first started this letter, weeks ago, I have thought back over the years you've been regrowing mentally. They contain so many thrilling, heartwarming experiences. In recalling them I have come to a startling realization. I wouldn't want to exchange these years for the normal, happy ones we no doubt would have had without the accident. Neither would I exchange the person you are today for the Sharon who at fifteen had above-average intelligence, and outstanding leadership qualities. I'm sure you are wondering why I would say a thing like that. I'm not sure I can explain it clearly, but I'll try.

I have the firm conviction that you can now fulfill a greater purpose in the world than you could have if you had matured normally. I hope what I write will help you realize that your severe injury has uniquely fitted you for service in areas where there is desperate need. Also I hope I can give you the sense of God's special hold on your life.

Without your injury, you would not belong to the handicapped groups that you attend regularly, and where you bring so much happiness. You carry on lively conversations with cerebral palsied persons whose words are unintelligible to me. The faces of crippled young men become radiant when you ''dance'' with them in wheelchairs, or laugh with them over some nonsense. The long telephone conversations you have with Sue, who can do so little except talk, and the way you constantly encourage Johnny to come out of his shell are examples of what I mean.

The sunshine you radiate isn't limited to handicapped persons, however. I'm sure you've brightened the outlook of many others by the remarks you make every time you have an opportunity—to friends, or to chance acquaintances on a city bus, in a store or classroom: ''I'm so fortunate that I'm not crippled or paralyzed. I can walk and run and go where I want to. I have so much to be thankful for.''

Your bright spirit is reflected also in your oil paintings, in their vivid colors and the way nature seems alive

144

on your canvasses. You have such an appreciation of beauty, and a real talent for art. Perhaps your pictures will brighten many homes in the future if you continue to work hard and learn all you can, and if you put your best effort into each painting.

The thought that should keep you striving with all your might is that God may use you to convince others that there is real hope for many severely brain-damaged persons—if they are given the right help. Doesn't it thrill you to think that you might be the means of bringing help to some of the thousands of persons now existing through years of vegetation in institutions?

Don't waste time thinking about what you might have been, but what you are capable of now—and the opportunities you have for the future. Your thoughts should be thrilling, happy ones, for you have the glorious opportunity and the unique abilities to bring hope and help to the hopeless, and to create beauty on canvas and in lives.

My sincere prayer is that you may let God guide you through a wonderfully bright, useful, and rewarding lifetime.

With deep love,
Mother

20

Rufus

DURING SHARON'S STAY at Easter Seal Camp in 1972 we received fewer phone calls than usual, and most of them seemed to center on one subject. "I sure want you to meet Rufus, Mother. He's one of the new counselors at camp. He's so nice. It's all right if he comes over the day after camp closes, isn't it? I'm sure you'll like him."

The gnawing uncertainty I experienced every time Sharon had a new male interest clouded my days. Past experience had taught me the necessity for extreme tact, patience, and faith. Even when I recognized an opportunist I knew I couldn't just say, "No, you can't let him come over, or go anyplace with him," without inciting rebellion. However, she did abide by the rule I insisted on—that before she make a date to go anyplace with a new friend, he must come to the house and I must have a chance to talk to him. A friendly chat, during which we discussed hobbies, religion, his type of employment,

Sharon's struggle since her accident, and our continued surveillance eliminated many prospective suitors.

She had dated a number of handicapped young men and several nonhandicapped ones who seemed to have a genuine, healthy interest in her, enjoyed her companionship, and showed a sincere desire to give her self-confidence. One, an excellent artist, came frequently to our home for more than a year. Sometimes he and Sharon went out to dinner, a movie, or a church activity, but often they just visited or watched television together here. He had left for the Merchant Marine shortly before Christmas.

Now I wondered what Rufus would be like. Paula, our daughter-in-law, met him when she visited Sharon at camp and reported with a puzzled, concerned expression on her face: "He talks to Sharon and about her as though she were perfectly normal."

I didn't say so, but I doubt if she could have told me anything about Rufus that would have impressed me more. I had long recognized the fact that Sharon yearned to be treated normally, not talked down to. Yet it seems to be an automatic reaction of persons in our society to consider anyone with any type of handicap to be on an inferior level. I realized how this distressed our daughter and others with related problems. I thought whatever else he might be like, Rufus evidently had the rare ability to discern Sharon's worth as an individual. I was looking forward to meeting him.

A few days later we picked Sharon up at camp. Her suitcases, sleeping bag, pillow, beach bag, laundry sack, and shoes had all been loaded into the trunk, and her daddy was urging her to get in so we could go, but she kept

148

stalling. Most of the handicapped had already left and she had exchanged numerous farewells with the few remaining ones. Still we waited. Suddenly she darted off and I saw a young man coming toward her. I watched as they walked arm in arm toward our car. He had short blond hair, a fair, sun-reddened complexion, and was several inches taller than Sharon. His eyes as he looked at our daughter held all the tender wonderment of budding love. As they approached the car Charley mumbled, "I don't like this."

"This is Rufus. This is my mom and dad."

"What is your last name?" Charley asked.

"Farrar. Rufus Farrar." They shook hands.

I told him: "Sharon has mentioned you in our phone conversations, and I'm glad to have the opportunity to meet you."

"I've been looking forward to meeting you also."

Their attention turned once more to each other, and they again seemed oblivious of our presence until Charley spoke, "Come on, Sharon, we have to go." She couldn't ignore his agitated tone, so after a few more precious minutes she climbed into the car.

"It's all right if I come over to see Sharon tomorrow, isn't it?" Rufus asked.

"Yes, that's OK, we'll see you tomorrow," I said.

Charley drove through the entrance and down the road a short distance before he voiced his thoughts, "You're headed for trouble."

His words echoed and reechoed in my mind during the following weeks. I knew Rufus and Sharon would ignore or defy any opposition to their romance. They talked over the phone for long periods each day, and spent his in-

149

THERE IS HOPE

frequent days off together. They went on picnics, played miniature golf, hiked, or just visited together in our home or his parents' home. Seeing them together left no doubt in my mind that they both felt sure they had found the one person in all the world uniquely made for them.

But I wasn't so sure. Was Sharon mature enough to be seriously in love? I knew so little about Rufus; was he right for our daughter? These and many other questions kept my mind in turmoil.

Then one night I awakened, suddenly, from deep sleep. Had someone called me? I listened, but heard nothing unusual. Charley's even breathing told me he was sleeping; no sound came from Sharon's room. It then seemed that my mind went blank, emptied of all thoughts, and into the void came four words, as though something within me spoke them: "Rufus is all right; Rufus is all right."

I lay still, my body tingling with awe and wonder; my soul listening. Soon I once more became aware of the usual night sounds, the hum of the refrigerator, the traffic on the nearby freeway. I knew the still small voice of God's guidance had completed His message.

Some months later I told Rufus about the experience, during one of the long talks we often had together. As he listened, his eyes mirrored the wonder I still felt. His voice had a reverent quality as he remarked, "I felt from the moment I met Sharon that God had brought us together."

"What was it that first attracted you to our daughter?" I asked.

"I think it was the way she responds to things. She feels nature, and her sparkling eyes and delighted expression make you enjoy it with her. She says 'how beautiful' from a deep sense of appreciation, not because it's the proper thing to say. There is a freshness and sincerity about her that I haven't found before.''

We discussed many things in our conversations; including things that I felt might present problems in their marriage. I told him I felt Sharon wouldn't be able to cope with the responsibility of children. He assured me that he realized this, and that it didn't make any difference in his desire to marry her.

Both Sharon and Rufus wanted to share the extreme happiness they had found with others who had a desperate need for companionship. In the months that followed they often took one or more handicapped persons along on their dates, to a show, or a picnic, or out to dinner.

In January, 1973, Sharon made her usual request when she got home from school. ''Come sit down and talk, Mom.''

I could tell by her excited manner that she had something special on her mind.

''I've decided on the date for our wedding, Mother. I want to be married on November 10.''

I sat speechless, too startled by her announcement to make any comment. Had I heard right? Did she really intend to be married on that date, the anniversary of her accident? She didn't seem to notice my reaction as she went on: ''You know, I've thought a lot about the fact that I wouldn't have met Rufus if I hadn't been struck by the car. I went to Easter Seal Camp because of my injury. So from now on instead of thinking of November 10 as a dreadful date, we're going to make it a day to celebrate.''

I gazed at the lovely young woman sitting there, her face reflecting the moving thoughts she'd just expressed. Then my thoughts went back to that black night brightened only by God's promise: "Sharon will live—she's going to be all right." Other memories flashed through my mind, with pictures of her during those long weeks when my hope almost withered. I reflected on how it slowly revived and grew steadily with her progress. Now hope had blossomed and was bearing wonderful fruit, for our brain-damaged child had become a young woman, with many handicaps to be sure, but with the ability to love and think deeply.

21

Another November 10

I AWOKE ON SATURDAY, NOVEMBER 10, to the sound of rain, which continued off and on all day. Like every bride, Sharon had hoped for sunshine, but there was more than enough inside to make up for the outside gloom.

When I entered the church dressing room that afternoon, the figure in the white bridal gown looked up, smiled and asked: "How do I look, Mom?"

"Lovely," I answered, and I thought, *Your outward beauty is enhanced by a radiant glow that comes from deep within and has its origin in 12 years of struggle. No wonder you are such a vision of loveliness!*

For weeks I'd been too busy to think. Now as I sat in the hushed atmosphere of the sanctuary, so many thoughts crowded my mind and stirred my emotions that I struggled to keep my composure. Dry-eyed, I watched Jeanne, Paula, and Sharon Norman walk down the aisle, beautiful in their orange dresses and wide-brimmed hats. Then came the first strains of the wedding march. As I looked back, watching for Sharon and her father, I caught sight of one of my closest friends, Kay Cruzic. The expression on her face held my gaze. Then I saw her lips quiver and tears start down her cheeks. My high resolve broke, and tears rolled down my cheeks, too, as I watched our daughter walk down the aisle to meet her husband.

I dabbed at them, and tried to concentrate on the minister's words. "Who gives this woman to be married to this man?"

"I do." Charley's voice sounded firm and steady. When he turned and walked to his place beside me, he was smiling and pride showed in his eyes.

I'm sure many others shed happy tears that afternoon. Later Paula commented, "I sensed an unusual atmosphere; the air was electric with emotion. It was as though each of those 225 guests had come to witness the result of a miracle."

I recalled those words many times as I observed the newlyweds in the months that followed. It was obvious that being husband and wife was sheer joy to both of them.

One day when they were visiting us Rufus remarked, "God has been so good to me. I'm so thankful He sent Sharon to me. She always seems so happy inside. I wish I could feel the way she does."

"Well, you know, for many years Sharon has had scores of people praying for her. No wonder she's happy."